ASSESSING MEDIA EDUCATION

LEA'S COMMUNICATION SERIES
Jennings Bryant / Dolf Zillmann, General Editors

Selected titles in media administration (William G. Christ, advisor) include:

Blanchard/Christ • *Media Education and the Liberal Arts: A Blueprint for the Profession*

Christ • Assessing *Media Education: A Resource Handbook for Educators and Administrators*

Christ • *Assessing Communication Education: A Handbook for Media, Speech, and Theatre Educators*

Christ • *Leadership in Times of Change: A Handbook for Communication and Media Administrators*

Dickson • *Mass Media Education in Transition: Preparing for the 21st Century*

For a complete list of titles in LEA's Communication Series, please contact Lawrence Erlbaum Associates, Publishers at www.erlbaum.com

ASSESSING MEDIA EDUCATION

A Resource Handbook
for Educators and Administrators

COMPONENT 2: CASE STUDIES

Edited by

William G. Christ
Trinity University

 LAWRENCE ERLBAUM ASSOCIATES, PUBLISHERS
2007   Mahwah, New Jersey   London

KH

This volume is an abridged version of *Assessing Media Education: A Resource Handbook for Educators and Administrators*, edited by William G. Christ. Additional components and the complete volume are available from Lawrence Erlbaum Associates, Inc. at www.erlbaum.com.

Lawrence Erlbaum Associates, Inc., Publishers
10 Industrial Avenue
Mahwah, New Jersey 07430
www.erlbaum.com

Cover design by Kathryn Houghtaling

Library of Congress Cataloging-in-Publication Data

Assessing media education : a resource handbook for educators and administrators / edited by William G. Christ.
    p. cm.
Includes bibliographical references and index.
ISBN 0-8058-6093-2 (cloth : alk. paper)
1. Mass media—Study and teaching (Higher)—Evaluation—Handbooks, manuals, etc.   I. Christ, William G.
P91.3.A853   2005
302.23'071'1—dc22   2005051015
                                                                CIP

Books published by Lawrence Erlbaum Associates are printed on acid-free paper, and their bindings are chosen for strength and durability.

Printed in the United States of America
10 9 8 7 6 5 4 3 2 1

10/19/06

Contents

Preface

Assessment is an integral part of what we do as teachers, researchers, and administrators. It can be formal or informal, systematic or haphazard, harmful or rewarding. At its best, assessment can have a transforming effect on education. At its worst, it can be used as an instrument to punish people and programs.

We are living in the age of accountability. Though calls for accountability and assessment have come and gone, the current demands for proving that students are learning seem more insistent as they become codified in educational policies. The move from asking teachers what they teach to requiring programs to show that students are learning is a paradigm shift that costs blood, sweat, and tears. It requires educators to look differently at their curricula, courses, syllabuses, and measurement mechanisms.

The purpose of this book is to provide useful information to those in higher education media programs who want to create or improve their student learning assessment strategies. This component, Part IV, in the main volume, provides case studies of programs at different points in their development of student outcomes.

If assessment is here to stay, then it is important for media educators to understand and use the process so that they control their own destinies. The hope is that this book will be a useful intellectual and practical resource for media educators and administrators as they grapple with the challenges of assessment.

ACKNOWLEDGMENTS

This book has been a very rewarding collaboration. I would like to publicly acknowledge the hard work of the authors involved in this project. Working with these authors has been a true pleasure. Their care and expertise will be evident to you as you read each chapter.

Second, I would like to thank the people at Lawrence Erlbaum Associates. Linda Bathgate was a major force behind the conceptualization and execution of this book. Nadine Simms has done a great job keeping the production side of the book on track. Tina Hardy did an excellent job as copy editor. The anonymous critiques of the early prospectus by conscientious reviewers made this a stronger book. I appreciate all their hard work.

From Trinity University, I would like to thank my department and the administration for their support. Trinity is an intellectually stimulating place where educational issues dealing with teaching, courses, and curricula are vigorously debated.

On a more personal note, I would like to thank those who developed the Internet and email. This project would have taken twice as long without these new communication technologies. I would also like to thank my sons Nathan and Jonathan Christ and especially my life partner, wife, and true friend, Judith Anne Christ.

Thank you one and all.

—*William G. Christ*
San Antonio, Texas

Component 2
Assessing Media Education
Case Studies

Introduction to Component 2

The chapters in this book are part of a larger book titled *Assessing Media Education: A Resource Handbook for Educators and Administrators*. This component is designed for those educators and administrators who need to know how other schools have grappled with assessment and have used assessment to improve their programs.

1

Introduction: Why Assessment Matters[1]

William G. Christ
Department of Communication
Trinity University

> *Accountability to my students meant: plan the course, show up in class, keep it moving, comment thoughtfully on papers, mentor when asked, submit grades, write recommendations—the usual packet of services. My obligation to my departmental colleagues: take on my share of core courses and administrative duties. To administrators and trustees: just don't make scenes, I guess; the thought rarely crossed my mind. My responsibility to society as a whole: I cheerfully held myself accountable for the wretched of the earth. . . .*
>
> —Ohmann (2000, p. 24)

If the programmatic assessment of student learning outcomes was universally acknowledged as being necessary, important, and positive, then it would not need to be defended. Yet, even those who accept the assessment of student learning outcomes in principle can find the job of planning, assessing, tabulating, and reporting so cumbersome and costly that they feel anger toward assessment efforts.

The assessment of student learning outcomes has become the acid test for media educators. It requires a paradigm shift in a faculty's thinking. Instead of focusing on traditional assessment "inputs" like faculty degrees, number of full-time faculty, research productivity, resources, facilities, equipment, diversity, and curriculum, a student learning ap-

---

[1]An earlier version of this chapter was in the Association of Schools of Journalism and Mass Communication *Insights* periodical.

proach to assessment focuses on "outputs." Instead of asking "what do faculty need to teach," the question becomes "what do we want students to learn?" "The question, 'What is basic about our discipline?' becomes 'What is basic about the discipline that students should learn and how do we know they have learned it?' " (Christ, McCall, Rakow, & Blanchard, 1997, p. 29).

Simply stated, faculty do assessment for either internal or external reasons. Yet, where we are in the assessment debates only makes sense within the broader context of off-campus forces impacting campuses. The first part of this chapter, therefore, outlines off-campus forces. Then, definitions are given and the two reasons are laid out.

OFF-CAMPUS FORCES

Jones, Jones, and Hargrove (2003) wrote that the first documented achievement tests can be linked to the mid-1800s when "the United States began an unprecedented effort to educate the masses" (p. 14). Janesick (2001, p. 89), who made a distinction between the testing movement (just after World War I) and the assessment movement, suggested that researchers should go back to the 1880s, "when Francis Galton, in London, administered tests to hundreds of persons to test sensory reactions and reaction times of volunteers," to understand the "big picture" of assessment. Both authors document the growth of public education after World War II and the transformative nature of the 1960s. Whereas Janesick argued that Howard Gardner's research on his theory of multiple intelligences almost "single-handedly starts the assessment movement" (p. 92), both researchers indicate the importance of the 1983 United States Department of Education's National Commission on Excellence in Education publication, "A Nation at Risk: The Imperative for Educational Reform" (1983), that "clearly situated public education as being in crisis and in need of major reform. The report used test scores as the indicator of success and the goal of schooling" (Jones et al., 2003, p. 15). The use of test scores as valid measures of excellence can be seen in the use of standardized tests like the Scholastic Assessment Test, American College Testing, and the Graduate Record Exam, and in the highly politicized "No Child Left Behind Act of 2001" (2002) legislation.

The Accountability Movement

Assessment is part of a larger accountability movement. Although it is clear from the previous discussion that accountability concerns are not new (see also Martin, Overholt, & Urban, 1976, pp. 33–41), Ohmann

(2000) has suggested that the current accountability movement grew out of three main forces in the late 1960s and early 1970s. The first "was an intense fiscal crisis of the state, brought on partly by war spending, but expressed chiefly as disillusionment with Great Society programs" (p. 28). Educational costs and expenditures had increased during the 1960s and there was concern that, as then deputy commissioner in the Office of Education Terrel H. Bell reported, "Money alone could not buy good education . . ." (p. 28).

Second, Ohmann (2000) argued that the accountability movement "was partly a counterthrust against liberatory ideas and experiments in 'open education,' that is, against the critique of schooling mounted by sixties visionaries and radicals" (p. 28). If the 1960s stood for student power, a democratization of higher education, and challenges to the educational status quo, then the rise of accountability in education could be seen as a direct challenge to these forces, suggesting to some that "traditional notions about the value of democracy and the value of the individual are ultimately at stake" (Martin et al., 1976, p. 6).

Finally, the third main force driving the accountability movement in education was a reaction against the "turmoil and disruption on the campuses; political action by students and faculty members . . . ; and mounting distrust of higher education by the public . . ." (Ohmann, 2000, p. 28). This led to "the increasing demand for colleges and universities to justify what they are doing and to disclose the effectiveness and efficiency of their operations" (McConnell, 1972, p. 200). Seen in this light, "one explanation for the failure of accountability advocates to heed objections by educators is that accountability is not primarily a pedagogical movement. It is an administrative system, and as such it is impervious to arguments which are based on educational concerns" (Martin et al., 1976, p. 32).

As the modern day accountability movement was building steam in the mid-1970s, there were a number of educators who wrote scathing critiques. Martin et al. (1976), in their critique of accountability in higher education, identified three major defects: "First, it lacks an adequate theoretical base" (p. 6). Accountability is a complex construct that is not always fully investigated and explicated by those who would use it (see Sarlos, 1973, pp. 65–81). Accountability tends to concentrate on behaviors and thus is informed by behavioral theory. Martin et al. argued that behavioral analysis limits education when they wrote, "because we believe that education has something to do with rational and critical thinking, introspection, and creativity, we believe that any view which confines itself exclusively to observable phenomena leaves out something essential both to the practice of science and to the process of education" (p. 6).

Besides the concern of a lack of an adequate theoretical base, basic questions dealing with accountability are not always answered. "For example, to contend that an individual or an institution ought to be accountable immediately brings to mind the questions: accountable to whom, for what, in what manner and under what circumstances?" (Wagner, 1989, p. 1). Other questions would include the following: Who should be held accountable (e.g., teachers, parents, school systems, school administrators, school teachers)? What does it mean to be accountable? When should accountability take place (e.g., grade level, proficiency level, every year)? What should be measured (e.g., knowledge, behavior, attitudes, values; see Part II)? How should accountability be measured (e.g., through portfolios, exit interviews, tests; see Part III)?

The second defect identified by Martin et al. (1976) was that accountability in education "lacks reassuring historical precedents. In fact, something very akin to accountability has been tried before and found wanting" (p. 6). They argued that the current push for accountability was only the most recent. Previous attempts had limited success.

"Third, its political implications are not reassuring to those among us who value either individuality or democracy" (Martin et al., 1976, p. 6). As stated previously, there are those who have argued that accountability, coming out of a business-training model, is not the best model for education. Bowers (1972) went so far as to argue that "teacher accountability is incompatible with academic freedom . . ." (p. 25).

[A]ccountability proponents could argue that despite various and sometimes conflicting interpretations of accountability there is at least general agreement about the following: (1) The quality of schools can no longer be determined simply by looking at input factors such as plant facilities, the number of volumes in the library, pupil/teacher ratios or printed curricula; rather, school performance and the quality of school programs are best understood in terms of results and output, what children do or do not learn over a given period; (2) learning can be measured against costs for a specified interval as an indication of cost-effectiveness; (3) taxpayers, parents and supportive government agencies have a "right" to know about these results and the cost/benefits associated with their schools; and (4) accountability can provide this information and act as a stimulus to better school performance. (Wagner, 1989, p. 2)

Whatever the historical roots of or problems with the current accountability and assessment movements, accountability and assessment appear here to stay. (For an overview of the assessment in higher education, see Rosenbaum, 1994.)

Forces Impacting Media Education

In the late 1980s and early 1990s, as the assessment movement continued to pick up steam (see Ervin, 1988; Ewell, Hutchings, & Marchese, 1991), at least three other challenges faced media education: calls for the reinvention of undergraduate education, the convergence of communication technologies, and the philosophical and theoretical ferment in the communication field (Blanchard & Christ, 1993; Dickson, 1995; Duncan, Caywood, & Newsom, 1993; "Planning for Curricular Change," 1984, 1987; Wartella, 1994).

It was argued that the reinvention of undergraduate education called for a "New Liberal Arts" that combined elements from both traditional and newer fields and disciplines (Blanchard & Christ, 1993). There were calls for a renewed commitment from media programs to the non-major, general student; a call for the centrality of media studies in the common curriculum of all students. As people debated what should be the outcome of an undergraduate education (see Association of American Colleges, 1985; Boyer, 1987; "Strengthening the Ties," 1988), media educators were faced with the following questions: What does my program have to offer the general university student? If one of the outcomes of a university education is to be media literate, then what should we teach and what should students learn? (see Christ & Potter, 1998).

The convergence of communication technologies and the philosophical and theoretical ferment in the communication field suggested there needed to be a new way of looking at the major. Some went so far as to demand a "New Professionalism" that educated students to become broad-based communication practitioners (Blanchard & Christ, 1993; see "Planning for Curricular Change," 1984, 1987). The calls for a broad approach to communication and media education has been both supported and attacked (see Dickson, 1995, 2000; Duncan et al., 1993; Medsger, 1996). The point is that the convergence of technologies and the philosophical and theoretical ferment in the field required media educators to reevaluate their programs to determine if what they offered made sense philosophically, pedagogically, and practically.

Overlaid on these three challenges was the assessment movement. As stated earlier, assessment, as part of the accountability movement, has been part of higher education for over 35 years. What is different now is the intensity of the current debate, where accrediting agencies seem to be taking the student learning assessment part of their charge very seriously and where legislators are willing to link funding to results. Assessment continues to be both a promise and a plague for programs as educators grapple with high expectations and limited resources (see Christ & Blanchard, 1994).

Student Learning

A report by the Kellogg Commission on the Future of State and Land-Grant Universities (1997) demonstrates how assessment dovetails with current calls for college and university reforms. The Kellogg Commission (1997) wanted to turn schools into learning institutions. They suggested "three broad ideals":

> (1) Our institutions must become *genuine learning communities*, supporting and inspiring faculty, staff, and learners of all kinds. (2) Our learning communities should be *student centered*, committed to excellence in teaching and to meeting the legitimate needs of learners, wherever they are, whatever they need, whenever they need it. (3) Our learning communities should emphasize the importance of *a healthy learning environment* that provides students, faculty, and staff with the facilities, support, and resources they need to make this vision a reality. (pp. v–vi, italics in original)

The move from universities being conceptualized as *teaching* institutions to *learning* institutions has profound implications for higher education (cf. Christ, 1994, 1997). As universities become more focused on student learning than on teaching, more concerned with the outcomes of education than the inputs into education, then at least two things become evident. First, outcomes assessment of learning becomes a "logical" important "next step" in the process, and second, the classroom is seen as only one part, and sometimes one small part, of the total learning environment.

The shift from teaching to learning communities, from teacher-centered to student-centered approaches to education, changes the role of the classroom teacher. If, as the Kellogg Commission (1997) suggested, learning communities should be committed "to meeting the legitimate needs of learners, wherever they are, whatever they need, whenever they need it" (pp. v–vi), then it is clear that teaching and learning can no longer be confined to the classroom. And, as the costs of higher education have escalated, as more people lose access to traditional higher education opportunities (Council for Aid to Education, 1997), the idea of a 4-year residential university or college, where lectures are delivered in huge classrooms, may become an anachronism. Within all of these challenges, educators are asked to assess their programs and student learning.

DEFINITIONS

So what is assessment? Krendl, Warren, and Reid (1997) made an interesting distinction between assessment and evaluation in their discussion about distant learning:

> Assessment refers to any process that measures what students have learned from teaching strategies, including course-specific methods (e.g., assignments, class activities, and tests) and programmatic strategies (e.g., exit interviews or honors theses) designed to test specific content knowledge. This primary focus on academic content is a defining characteristic of student assessment. Evaluation, on the other hand, looks beyond this to examine the entire educational experience. The mesh between students' needs and their experiences during a course or program is the primary criterion in evaluation. Beyond teaching strategies, then, evaluation examines classroom interaction, the effectiveness of course/program administration, the quality of student support services, access to and quality of technical equipment, and cost-benefit analyses of distance-education programs. In short, every aspect of a distance course or program can be evaluated, whereas only students' mastery of course content is assessed (Rowntree, 1992). (p. 103)

The distinction between assessment and evaluation is useful in that it directs our attention to different levels or types of accountability. Haley and Jackson (1995) suggested a hierarchy of programmatic assessment that included four levels, where

> each level may be seen as a broader examination of the program. The four levels are: Level One—Evaluation of individual program components <peer teaching review and course evaluations>; Level Two—Perceptions and performance of graduating students <survey of seniors; senior essays; university comprehensives; departmental comprehensives; campaigns courses>; Level Three—Evaluations of key internal and external constituencies <faculty surveys; employer surveys; university alumni surveys; department graduate surveys>; and Level Four—Comprehensive program evaluation <program review; accreditation>. (p. 27)

Student learning outcomes assessment is normally positioned as a level-four programmatic evaluation. Of course, to do assessment is not easy. Morse and Santiago (2000) wrote that, "to evaluate student learning adequately, faculty must set programmatic goals, understand the profiles of students, define the desired outcomes for students and programs, develop instruments to measure those outcomes, and establish a feedback loop in which the information gained is used to effective positive change" (p. 33).

WHY ASSESSMENT?

There are two fundamental reasons for assessment. The first is external and the second is internal.

External

As mentioned earlier, demand for assessment grew out of calls for accountability. "House (1993) proposed three different types of accountability that institutions of higher education face: state- or public-controlled accountability, professional control (by professors and administrators), and consumer control" (Krendl et al., 1997, p. 109). These three types of accountability are external to the media unit and are often seen by the unit as being harmful, coercive, or irrelevant. Under these conditions, assessment, at its best, might be seen as an antidote to calls for accountability. For example, "Lombardi (1993) posits, 'To counter-attack against criticism from the public, we need to explain and teach the public what the universities do, how they do it, and why it costs so much . . . The key weapon here is accounting' " (Haley & Jackson, 1995, p. 33). In other words, assessment is seen as a weapon to be used by the beleaguered unit to answer criticisms.

The first reason for doing assessment is that certain states, regional accrediting agencies, local administrators, professional accrediting groups, parents, and students have called for or mandated assessment. If state legislatures have developed carrots and sticks based on assessment and results, then that is an excellent reason why a unit would want to do assessment. If a unit wants to be either regionally or professionally accredited and it needs to evaluate its program and student learning outcome as part of the process, then this is an excellent reason for doing assessment. If an administration says to develop an assessment plan, then this, too, is an excellent reason for doing assessment. Ideally, a unit will be able to turn the often-odious chore of assessment into a well-articulated persuasive argument about needs and expectations. Hopefully, a unit will be able to transform all its hard work into a plan for how to improve what it does. And hopefully, a unit will be given the resources to help improve its program.

Internal

The second reason to do assessment is that it has the potential to make teachers, programs, and ultimately, students, better. Assessment can help a unit be self-reflective about what is done and why it is done. It can mean discovering the strengths and weaknesses of programs and the teaching and learning process. "Assessment is an integral part of what we do as teachers, researchers, and administrators. It can be formal or informal, systematic or haphazard, harmful or rewarding. At its best, assessment can have a transforming effect on education. At its worst, it can be used as an instrument to punish people and programs" (Christ, 1994, p. x).

SUMMARY

This book presents four case studies of schools in different phases of developing assessment plans and using those plans to improve their programs. It is important that an assessment plan should link a university's mission statement with the program's mission that should confirm the program's core values, competencies, and knowledge. These core values, competencies, and knowledge should be linked to student learning outcomes which are clearly present in programs' curricula and courses and even exercises and experiences within courses. Once the student learning outcomes are articulated, then both indirect and direct methods can be developed to continually assess the outcomes. Finally, the results from the assessment should be fed back into the system.

CONCLUSION

Ultimately, there is good assessment and bad assessment. Bad assessment is when, through lack of time, resources or will, tests or measures are thrown together to appease some outside agency or administrator. Good assessment is assessment that helps teachers and programs improve what they do so that teachers can teach and students can learn better. The American Association for Higher Education (AAHE Assessment Forum, 1997) suggests nine key "principles of good practice for assessing student learning":

1. The assessment of student learning begins with educational values; 2. Assessment is most effective when it reflects an understanding of learning as multidimensional, integrated, and revealed in performance over time; 3. Assessment works best when the programs it seeks to improve have clear, explicitly stated purposes; 4. Assessment requires attention to outcomes but also and equally to the experiences that lead to those outcomes; 5. Assessment works best when it is ongoing, not episodic; 6. Assessment fosters wider improvement when representatives from across the educational community are involved; 7. Assessment makes a difference when it begins with issues of use and illuminates questions that people really care about; 8. Assessment is most likely to lead to improvement when it is part of a

larger set of conditions that promote change; 9. Through assessment, educators meet responsibilities to students and to the public. (pp. 11-12)

After evaluating a trial batch of student learning assessment plans from a number of Journalism and Mass Communication programs who were coming up for accreditation, the AEJMC Teaching Standards Committee (Hansen, 2004) suggested the following:

1. Assessment plans should include the unit's mission statement.
2. Assessment plans should include the "professional values and competencies" all students must master, and plans should be revised to insure they conform to the final, approved language for the "professional values and competencies" as stated in ACEJMC's . . . Accreditation Standards.
3. Assessment plans should address the means by which students will be made aware of the "professional values and competencies" as they move through the program and the major.
4. Assessment plans should reflect the concept of different levels of student learning (awareness, understanding and application). The methods used to assess student learning should indicate the level at which students are expected to perform. For example, if a direct measure is being used to evaluate student mastery of the competency of writing correctly and clearly, the measurement method should reflect the level of performance expected (most likely "application" for that competency).
5. Assessment plans should clearly identify which methods are deemed to be direct and which are deemed to be indirect measures of student learning.
6. Assessment plans should clearly link the method for measuring student learning with the appropriate "professional values and competencies" that are expected to be measured through that method.
7. Assessment plans should address the "indicators" that are articulated in Standard 9 of the new Accrediting Standards to ensure that appropriate evidence is provided for site team visitors.
8. Assessment plans should specifically articulate how the assessment effort will be staffed and maintained so that assessment is ongoing.
9. Assessment plans should specifically detail how the data collected from the direct and indirect measures will be used to improve curriculum and instruction over time.

Assessment did not just happen. It has developed within a complex of powerful forces that have continued to impact higher education. Why assessment matters is a function of both external constituencies and internal needs. The bottom line is that it is useful for media educators to address the questions: What do we want to be able to say about our students when they graduate from our program? Why do we teach what we teach? And, for assessment purposes, how do we know our students are learning what we are teaching? Hopefully, this book will help generate a discussion that will help us answer these questions.

REFERENCES

Accrediting Council on Education in Journalism and Mass Communications. (2004). *New accrediting standards.* Retrieved July 24, 2004, from http://www.ukans.edu/~acejmc/BREAKING/New_standards_9-03.pdf

American Association for Higher Education Assessment Forum. (1997). *9 principles of good practice for assessing student learning.* Retrieved March 25, 2005, from http://www.aahe.org/assessment/principl.htm

Association of American Colleges. (1985). *Integrity in the college curriculum: A report to the academic community.* Washington, DC: Author.

Blanchard, R. O., & Christ, W. G. (1993). *Media education and the liberal arts: A blueprint for the new professionalism.* Hillsdale, NJ: Lawrence Erlbaum Associates, Inc.

Bowers, C. A. (1972). Accountability from a humanist point of view. In F. J. Sciara & R. K. Jantz (Eds.), *Accountability in American education* (pp. 25–33). Boston: Allyn & Bacon.

Boyer, E. L. (1987). *College: The undergraduate experience in America.* New York: The Carnegie Foundation for the Advancement of Teaching, Harper & Row.

Christ, W. G. (Ed.). (1994). *Assessing communication education.* Hillsdale, NJ: Lawrence Erlbaum Associates, Inc.

Christ, W. G. (Ed.). (1997). *Media education assessment handbook.* Mahwah, NJ: Lawrence Erlbaum Associates, Inc.

Christ, W. G., & Blanchard, R. O. (1994). Mission statements, outcomes and the new liberal arts. In W. G. Christ (Ed.), *Assessing communication education* (pp. 31–55). Hillsdale, NJ: Lawrence Erlbaum Associates, Inc.

Christ, W. G., McCall, J. M., Rakow, L., & Blanchard, R. O. (1997). Integrated communication programs. In W. G. Christ (Ed.), *Media education assessment handbook* (pp. 23–53). Mahwah, NJ: Lawrence Erlbaum Associates, Inc.

Christ, W. G., & Potter, W. J. (1998). Media literacy, media education, and the academy. *Journal of Communication, 48*(1), 5–15.

Council for Aid to Education. (1997). *Breaking the social contract. The fiscal crisis in higher education.* Retrieved March 25, 2005, from http://www.rand.org/publications/CAE/CAE100/index.html

Dickson, T. (1995, August). *Meeting the challenges and opportunities facing media education: A report on the findings of the AEJMC Curriculum Task Force.* Paper presented at the annual convention of the Association for Education in Journalism and Mass Communication, Washington, DC.

Dickson, T. (2000). *Mass media education in transition.* Mahwah, NJ: Lawrence Erlbaum Associates, Inc.

Duncan, T., Caywood, C., & Newsom, D. (1993, December). *Preparing advertising and public relations students for the communications industry in the 21st century.* A report of the Task Force on Integrated Curriculum.

Ervin, R. F. (1988). Outcomes assessment: The rationale and the implementation. In R. L. Hoskins (Ed.), *Insights* (pp. 19–23). Columbia, SC: Association of Schools of Journalism and Mass Communication.

Ewell, P. T., Hutchings, P., & Marchese, T. (1991). *Reprise 1991: Reprints of two papers treating assessment's history and implementation*. Washington, DC: American Association for Higher Education, Assessment Forum.

Haley, E., & Jackson, D. (1995). A conceptualization of assessment for mass communication programs. *Journalism and Mass Communication Educator, 51,* 26–34.

Hansen, K. (2004). *Accreditation guidelines for evaluating assessment of student learning plans* (Memorandum sent by the Committee on Teaching Standards chair to the chair of the Accrediting Council on Education in Journalism and Mass Communication accrediting committee).

House, E. (1993). *Professional evaluation*. Newbury Park, CA: Sage.

Janesick, V. J. (2001). *The assessment debate*. Santa Barbara, CA: AGC-CLIO, Inc.

Jones, M. G., Jones, B. D., & Hargrove, T. Y. (2003). *The unintended consequences of high-stakes testing*. Lanham, MD: Rowman & Littlefield Publishers, Inc.

Kellogg Commission on the Future of State and Land-Grant Universities. (1997). *Returning to our roots: The student experience*. Retrieved March 25, 2005, from http://www.nasulgc.org/publications/Kellogg/Kellogg2000_StudentExp.pdf

Krendl, K. A., Warren, R., & Reid, K. A. (1997). Distance learning. In W. G. Christ (Ed.), *Assessing communication education* (pp. 99–119). Mahwah, NJ: Lawrence Erlbaum Associates, Inc.

Lombardi, V. (1993). With their accounts in order, colleges can win back their critics. *The Chronicle of Higher Education, 39,* A40.

Martin, D. T., Overholt, G. E., & Urban, W. J. (1976). *Accountability in American education: A critique*. Princeton, NJ: Princeton Book Company.

McConnell, T. R. (1972). Accountability and autonomy. In F. J. Sciara & R. K. Jantz (Eds.), *Accountability in American education* (pp. 200–214). Boston: Allyn & Bacon.

Medsger, B. (1996). *Winds of change: Challenges confronting journalism education*. Arlington, VA: The Freedom Forum.

Morse, J. A., & Santiago, G., Jr. (2000). Accreditation and faculty. *Academe, 86*(1), 30–34.

National Commission on Excellence in Education. (1983). *A nation at risk: The imperative for educational reform*. Retrieved March 25, 2005, from http://www.ed.gov/pubs/NatAtRisk/index.html

No Child Left Behind Act of 2001. (2002). Public law 107-110. January 8, 2002. Retrieved March 25, 2005, from http://www.ed.gov/policy/elsec/leg/esea02/index.html

Ohmann, R. (2000). Historical reflections on accountability. *Academe, X,* 24–29.

Planning for curricular change in journalism education. (1984). *The Oregon Report* (Project on the Future of Journalism and Mass Communication Education). Eugene: University of Oregon, School of Journalism.

Planning for curricular change in journalism education (2nd ed.). (1987). The Oregon Report. (Project of the Future of Journalism and Mass Communication Education). Eugene: University of Oregon, School of Journalism.

Rosenbaum, J. (1994). Assessment: An overview. In W. G. Christ (Ed.), *Assessing communication education: A handbook for media, speech, and theatre educators* (pp. 3–29). Hillsdale, NJ: Lawrence Erlbaum Associates, Inc.

Rowntree, D. (1992). *Exploring open and distance learning*. London: Kogan Page.

Sarlos, B. (1973). The complexity of the concept 'accountability' in the context of American education. In R. L. Leight (Ed.), *Philosophers speak on accountability in education* (pp. 65–81). Danville, IL: Interstate.

Strengthening the ties that bind: Integrating undergraduate liberal and professional study (Report of the Professional Preparation Network). (1988). Ann Arbor: The Regents of the University of Michigan.

Wagner, R. B. (1989). *Accountability in education: A philosophical inquiry.* New York: Routledge.

Wartella, E. (1994). Foreword. In *State of the field: Academic leaders in journalism, mass communication and speech communication look to the future at the University of Texas* (p. 1). Austin: The University of Texas at Austin, College of Communication.

22

University of Minnesota

Kathleen A. Hansen
School of Journalism and Mass Communication
University of Minnesota

The earlier chapters in this volume have reviewed the process of developing assessment plans, articulating appropriate outcomes in journalism and mass communication curricula, and devising student learning outcomes measures. This chapter describes the assessment process as it has been applied at the University of Minnesota School of Journalism and Mass Communication, and focuses particularly on the ways that process has been useful in examining the curriculum.

THE UNIVERSITY OF MINNESOTA UNDERGRADUATE PROGRAM

The School of Journalism and Mass Communication (SJMC) is a unit within the College of Liberal Arts (CLA) at the University of Minnesota. Hence, students take the majority of their coursework in subject areas outside the journalism and mass communication major and must meet the liberal education coursework requirements set by the CLA. Many journalism students carry a double major or a minor in areas such as Political Science, English, History, Psychology, or similar liberal arts subjects.

The SJMC administers a secondary admissions process to limit enrollment in the program. The SJMC has more than 1,300 undergraduate majors, premajors, and minors—the second-largest enrollment in the CLA. To manage demand for seats in courses and to allow students the opportunity to actually finish their requirements in 4 years, the SJMC processes student applications three times a year, admitting approxi-mately 375 to 400 students each year in total. Enrollment in skills courses (reporting, copywriting, editing, etc.) is limited to 16 to 20 students in a section. Multiple sections of these courses are offered each semester and in the summer session to meet student demand.

The SJMC admits undergraduate students into one of three tracks—journalism, strategic communication, and mass communication. The journalism track encompasses all media "channels"—newspapers, magazines, television, online, photojournalism. The strategic communication track encompasses advertising and public relations (PR). The mass communication track is reserved for students who do not intend to work in a mass communication profession, but who want to study mass communication processes and effects in a liberal arts context.

The SJMC abolished traditional "sequences" many years ago. Students in the program take two required courses in common—an introduction to mass communication class and a class on information gathering and evaluation. After that common core of courses, students branch off into their respective track coursework, working in close consultation with their faculty advisers to choose the appropriate courses for their specialization. All students in the journalism and strategic communication tracks are required to take a combination of skills and "context" courses (history, law, social processes, etc.), but most of the specific courses beyond the core are not prescribed. Each student program is tailored to the interests and goals of the individual. Students in the journalism and strategic communication tracks are required, however, to complete at least one "capstone" course in their area as part of their skills course mix.

Mass communication track students take context courses for the bulk of their work in the SJMC. Their "capstone" experience consists of advanced courses in media history, law, social effects, new media, and so forth. They do not produce professional projects as do the students in the professional tracks. Instead, they write traditional academic papers that demonstrate their mastery of the core concepts in the mass communication field.

As mentioned, students work with SJMC faculty advisers. The faculty (21 tenured or tenure-track members, 3 teaching specialists) take their advising responsibilities seriously and meet with students individually to design their program plans. A journalism track program might consist of the two required core courses, a basic reporting and writing course, a publications editing course, several advanced reporting courses (by subject or "channel"), a journalism history course, a media law course, a media and popular culture course, and a new media economics course. A strategic communication track program might consist of the two required courses, an introduction to PR course, a PR writing and tactics course, a strategic communication research course, a media graphics course, a strategic communication cases course, a campaigns course, a media law course, a media and society course, a public opinion formation course, and an international communications course. The journalism track student's "capstone" course might be Advanced Electronic News Writing and Reporting. The strategic communication track student's capstone course would be Strategic Communication Campaigns.

The Twin Cities provide a rich media market with many adjunct instructors (30+ per year) teaching skills courses for the SJMC. The advantage of having such a wealth of adjunct instructors is that students have a chance to interact with top professionals who are practicing their craft and sharing their knowledge with the next generation of media practitioners. The disadvantage is that any plan to assess student learning must take into account the time constraints of adjunct instructors and the part-time nature of their engagement with the curriculum. Extensive coordination of and consultation with adjunct instructors is necessary for any assessment plan to succeed.

Another challenge is that despite the University of Minnesota–Twin Cities (U of M) role as the state's flagship, land grant, Carnegie 1 research university with a full complement of undergraduate, graduate, and professional schools and programs, many students treat the U of M as a "commuter" campus and attend school part time. Most majors in the SJMC work at least 25 hr a week in addition to attending classes, and most support themselves rather than rely on parents' financial resources. Unlike those at residential campuses in smaller communities, students at the U of M have a thousand and one things to do besides being full-time students. This makes it difficult to develop an assessment plan that might, for instance, require every student to undertake an unpaid internship or complete a practicum. The reality of many students' lives is that they simply don't have the time or financial ability to do so.

PROCESS OF DEVELOPING AN ASSESSMENT PLAN

Following the Accrediting Council on Education in Journalism and Mass Communications' (ACEJMC) establishment of a Fall 2003 deadline for all schools to have an assessment plan in place, the SJMC assembled a special task force of three faculty members focused on outcomes assessment. That task force met regularly during Fall 2002 to discuss the existing evaluation options, how the rest of the faculty should be consulted, and what additional conversations would be useful to engage individuals both inside and outside the U of M. Those conversations brought good and bad news: Many people in the CLA and at fellow ACEJMC-member institutions were happy to discuss these issues, but a survey of similar programs quickly revealed that little progress had been made anywhere as of that date.

In the Fall of 2002, all faculty were asked to complete an assessment matrix or grid for every course they teach (see Appendix A, which articulates the ACEJMC "Professional Values and Competencies"). Faculty were asked to indicate which of the 11 core values and competencies outlined by ACEJMC were included in their courses, and whether their coverage of those values and competencies was at the awareness, understanding, or application level. Faculty submitted these grids to the task force and all data were entered into a database. One faculty meeting in the Fall was devoted to a discussion of the findings of that analysis.

The SJMC Director also asked all faculty to develop course learning objectives for each course they teach (see Appendix B). Up until that time, faculty were not required to include course learning objectives on their syllabi. These learning objectives were collected by the Director and passed along to the task force. The task force asked all faculty to start including course learning objectives on their syllabi. In addition, the Undergraduate Committee was asked to begin a systematic review of the entire undergraduate curriculum based on the information from the assessment grids and the course learning objective projects.

Also in the Fall of 2002, the members of the task force reviewed the latest assessment literature (see Appendix D), developed an initial draft of all possible assessment options, and presented these to the faculty. Based on the feedback and discussion of all options, the members of the task force were directed to seek assistance from outside the SJMC in paring down the list of options to something manageable and feasible.

In Spring 2003, members of the task force met with a U of M evaluation expert from the Office of Educational Policy and Administration and learned that a number of important evaluation resources already existed on campus, including archived student course evaluation data, software applications for collecting student work, and a system to evaluate capstone course student work that was amenable to cohort evaluation. The task force decided to build on those existing resources to develop a revised plan that incorporated the measures and strategies that were considered most useful for our curriculum and most likely to be sustainable.

Also in the Spring of 2003, task force members consulted with Dean Trevor Brown of Indiana University, who chaired the ACEJMC Standards and Assessment Committee. Dean Brown reviewed the options under consideration for our plan and provided extensive feedback on each in light of the Committee's discussion about assessment to that point.

After review of all the information collected throughout the 2002 to 2003 academic year, the task force members wrote another draft of the assessment plan. This draft of the assessment plan was shared with the CLA Associate Dean for Academic Programs for feedback and review before presentation to the faculty. The Associate Dean suggested several additional resources that might prove helpful, and offered to provide assistance in implementing one element of the assessment plan (use of the university's "Portfolio" software system) in the form of naming the SJMC as a "pilot case" for that program. She also expressed gratitude that the SJMC was going through this process because the North Central Association of Colleges and Schools will require all accredited universities to implement an assessment program in the next review, and the Associate Dean is responsible for assisting CLA units in developing their plans. She said she would look to the SJMC as a model for developing and implementing such plans in departments and units throughout the CLA.

Aside from material resources, the SJMC also already possessed, prior to this evaluation plan development, a key intellectual resource: namely, a mission statement that provides a concrete sense of what the faculty want to accomplish with their work. That mission statement was central to our plan. The importance of a well-articulated mission statement to the assessment process is discussed elsewhere in this volume.

All of this work during the 2002 to 2003 academic year informed the development of the assessment plan. Much work remained to be completed by the time the Fall 2003 ACEJMC deadline for having a plan in place arrived. Our plan included a number of suggestions for additional information collection, development of measurement tools, and continuous work in evaluating the curriculum. The plan reflects the fact that assessment needs to be ongoing, systematic, and flexible enough to respond to changing circumstances.

The key elements of the assessment plan at the U of M include the direct measures of a capstone course project assessment process, and a process for reviewing student portfolios of work using the "Portfolio" software system. The indirect measures in the SJMC's plan include a review of course learning objectives over time, a review of student course evaluation data over time, and a special emphasis on demographics that will track students of color as they move through the program and provide help and support where necessary to ensure a high graduation rate.

BENEFITS OF THE PROCESS

Mission Statement Revision

The faculty voted to revise the SJMC's mission statement to incorporate the 11 core values and competencies articulated by ACEJMC. The mission statement had been expressed entirely in terms of "inputs"—that is, the statement articulated the SJMC's goals for the type of curriculum we were committed to delivering. By revising the mission statement to incorporate the student learning "outcomes" of the ACEJMC core values and competencies, the mission statement now brought the two sets of goals—inputs and outcomes—together for the first time.

Curriculum Review

With a revised mission statement in hand, the members of the Undergraduate Committee started reviewing the entire curriculum in light of the ACEJMC values and competencies. As discussed, each faculty member completed an assessment grid that identified whether and at what level the courses they teach address any of the 11 values and competencies. Responses from all faculty were compiled into a summary spreadsheet to see larger patterns or gaps. By analyzing these results, the Committee learned, for instance, that very few courses in the curriculum focused on the competencies necessary for students to master the application of basic numerical and statistical concepts. This analysis helped the Committee see where the journalism, strategic communication, and mass communication tracks had both strengths and weaknesses in helping students master the 11 core values and competencies.

The data from faculty responses also helped identify specific courses in the curriculum on which the Undergraduate Committee should focus. For instance, different faculty responses for separate sections of a specific course were quite divergent, depending on how a faculty member conceptualized the course and what types of teaching materials (texts, assignment books, etc.) were being used in each section. The Committee used these results to help the faculty teaching those sections to work together to better coordinate separate sections of the same course.

Course and Track Revisions

In light of these discrepancies, the Undergraduate Committee's work with the course syllabi for the entire curriculum was especially important. The Committee focused on reviewing the course objectives that all course syllabi were to incorporate. One of the Committee's goals was to bring course objectives into alignment across sections and instructors. Another goal was to determine whether the courses in a professional track, as a whole, exposed students to the 11 core values and competencies at the appropriate level. Members of the Committee met with faculty teaching in the three tracks to help them review all the courses in their area in light of the assessment grid data to look for overlap, gaps, and possible ways to revise the curriculum to be sure all 11 values and competencies were being covered at some point in a student's program.

Capstone Course Project Assessment

In addition to reviewing the assessment grid data and all course objectives, the Undergraduate Committee worked with individual faculty members teaching the "capstone" courses to start developing course project assessment methods. Most capstone courses in the journalism and strategic communication tracks have students develop a course project. These had been evaluated solely by the faculty teaching the course. Going forward, on a biannual basis, someone other than the instructor will be asked to serve as the evaluator of a sample of student projects. This may be done at the same time as the student presentations of their projects during class time.

Assessment Rubrics

In Fall 2003, all current instructors for SJMC capstone professional courses were invited to participate in sessions to produce a standard form, or "rubric," for assessment of capstone projects in their area (either strategic communication or one of several journalism specializations). Rubrics were tailored specifically to each capstone course and the types of projects students produce, and were designed to be applied by "outsiders" who were not the primary instructors (see Appendix C). Some faculty decided to share the rubrics with students at the outset as part of the instructions for successfully completing projects. Others use the rubrics as a grading feedback resource. In any case, developing the rubrics helped faculty clarify goals for student projects.

The plan at the time of this writing is to ask a pilot group of invited judges to use the rubric forms as measures of their evaluation of selected capstone projects developed in the Fall 2004 semester. If such forms generally are useful to the array of invited judges, the SJMC will adopt them as a standard form for distribution and use in any invited review of capstone projects.

Using the U's "Portfolio" Software

The other major direct measure was the use of "Portfolio" software. This software encourages students to build portfolios of their course projects and assignments as they move through the major. The software is available to all U of M students and faculty and allows students to collect 20 megabytes of material in one location. The software provides secure access to authorized users only and can store text, images, video, and other sorts of production work (it is available at http://portfolio. umn.edu).

Starting in the 2003 to 2004 academic year, all faculty were encouraged to require students to post their relevant assignments or projects in the "Portfolio" system. Instructors teaching Jour 3004, Information for Mass Communication, the required first course students take as new majors, introduce students to this system and require them to post their course major projects so all students have familiarity with the system as they proceed to their more advanced courses.

The Undergraduate Committee and members of the task force worked throughout the 2003 to 2004 academic year to develop a method to sample student portfolio entries for evaluation of student learning and to develop the measurement tools for assessment of student work. A group of SJMC faculty and outside evaluators will periodically review this sample of student work and apply measures of the course learning objectives and core values and competencies in the professional tracks and the mass communication track. For example, outside evaluators may be allowed access to materials in the portfolios of a set of beginning students, and to those of a set of students ready to graduate. The evaluators might be asked to "sort" the students' portfolios based on their perceived level of mastery of the "writing" competency. A "good" assessment outcome would, obviously, be one that placed the advanced students' work in the highest category.

Future Curriculum Discussions Framed Through Assessment Lens

Perhaps one of the most important benefits of developing the assessment plan was that the entire faculty was engaged in a discussion of the core values and competencies of our field and how our curriculum measured up. A curriculum is a constantly-evolving entity, and the latest evolution has now incorporated explicit goals and outcomes for student learning. No one on the faculty can imagine undertaking any future curriculum or course development project that doesn't include this assessment perspective as an important element to consider.

Student Awareness of Core Values and Competencies

As a result of the assessment project, all students are now aware of the core competencies and values of their intended professions and areas of study because they have been included on course syllabi in the very first courses students take in the major and on all other syllabi throughout the curriculum. Advisers working with students newly admitted into the major can use the ACEJMC competencies and values as a "road map" to explain to students the logic of their course choices. A number of faculty have expressed their delight in being able to discuss with students in their classes the important characteristics of the mass communication field and professions through reference to the ACEJMC principles.

In addition to the 11 core values and competencies any well-educated journalism and mass communication major should master, all students now know the specific course objectives for each course in the SJMC curriculum. It may be hard to imagine, but the SJMC had no requirement for faculty to include course objectives on syllabi before this assessment project started. Many faculty, of course, included objectives on their syllabi on their own initiative, and many developed specific objectives for individual assignments and projects. However, there was no uniform model for developing and articulating course objectives, and no process for comparing objectives across courses and throughout a specific track. The assessment process has exposed all faculty to the best practices for developing course and learning objectives, and has provided students with a clear outline of the materials they should expect to master by taking any given course.

New Faculty Knowledge

In addition, faculty have updated and expanded their familiarity with assessment best practices, trends in the field, and how sister institutions are innovating in the assessment arena. Middle-level and senior faculty at most institutions joined the academy at a time when there was little attention paid to developing stellar teachers. If one had the right academic credentials and brought the promise of producing important scholarship to a teaching position, that was deemed enough. That has obviously changed in many places, certainly for the better. But senior faculty have not necessarily had a chance to catch up. The assessment process has given senior faculty a way to engage with the literature of teaching and learning without feeling stigmatized or being asked, "Why don't you know this already if you've been teaching all these years?" Because everyone was declared to be in the same situation—in need of a crash course on the most recent and best thinking in the student learning assessment field—it provided a way for the entire faculty to bring their skills up to speed together.

Common Language

Faculty teaching sections of the same course and within a professional track now have a common language to discuss student learning goals, objectives, and teaching strategies. In addition, faculty can examine all the courses in the track with an eye toward developing course content to ensure that students have the most complete and comprehensive exposure to the field as possible, using the 11 core values and competencies as the guide. The Undergraduate Committee, in concert with the faculty teaching in the area, has targeted several courses in the curriculum for revision based on the "gaps" the assessment process exposed. We all know that discussions among faculty about course content, coverage, and approaches can be fraught with trouble—ego defensiveness, claims of abridgements of academic freedom, turf battles. The assessment process provides a nonthreatening way for "outsiders" (those who don't teach a specific course) to examine and influence course content without appearing to overstep boundaries.

Clarifying Goals and Reenergizing Faculty

The assessment process has also helped the faculty clarify course goals, teaching priorities, and grading criteria for their own courses. The discussions about new ways to engage students and assess student learning have reenergized many faculty and provided an impetus to try new things and revise tried-and-true things with new twists. For instance, faculty teaching the capstone magazine production and editing course discovered through the "rubric creation" process that they had not been clearly articulating several project evaluation standards to the students. They realized that was the reason students had problems meeting their expectations for that part of the course project work. Being "forced" to create explicit criteria for assigning below average, average, above average, or excellent assessments to the work helped the instructors revise the instructions to students about how to do the work in the first place. The faculty who have developed the rubrics for the capstone courses, in particular, have expressed amazement at how the exercise clarified their thinking.

Students Understand Expectations

Students have benefited from improved project or assignment assessment processes. They now have a clear set of expectations and a clear

statement of how well (or how inadequately) they've met those expectations. Rather than assigning a letter grade or a set of points with a few
written comments to help the students understand the score, faculty
can now provide students with a concrete list of expectations and an
explanation for why something did not measure up or was judged supe-
rior to others' work.

Documenting Outcomes

Faculty have also realized the need to focus on documenting their students' accomplishments. Most universities require faculty to document
their research, teaching, and service activities each year. Prior to the assessment project work, faculty in the SJMC documented their teaching
accomplishments by sharing course syllabi and assignments, by including student course evaluations in the file, perhaps by asking a peer to sit
in on a class or two to prepare a peer teaching observation report for
the file, and by other similar methods. Most of these focused on the "inputs" of teaching—"here is what I say I'm doing, here are the assignments I've developed to accomplish my goals, here are the views of my
colleagues as to my teaching technique and mastery of the classroom
setting." None of the evidence, save the student course evaluations
(which do not assess student learning except by self-report with one
question), address the outcomes of teaching. The assessment project
has required the faculty to focus on how they might explicitly demonstrate student learning as a result of having been exposed to the teaching inputs. That means faculty have to look at what they are doing from
a very different part of the process.

Many faculty realized as they reviewed assessment techniques and
practices that they had been doing student learning assessment in their
courses, but they had not been collecting or analyzing those results. For
instance, a number of faculty reported that they regularly started their
courses with an informal "exam" that attempted to gauge student familiarity with the central course concepts and knowledge areas. They
would reexamine student knowledge (outside the context of a formal
course exam) as the course progressed throughout the semester. This is
a form of student learning assessment, obviously. But no one who was
doing this regularly archived or analyzed those "exams" or thought they
would have any value except as guidance for the faculty themselves to
adjust course content based on feedback from students about their
teaching. Once the faculty discussed using these types of techniques to
document student learning, it was clear that many faculty would start
collecting and analyzing that material with a new perspective on the
value such things have for assessment.

Engaging Faculty in Total Curriculum Planning

Another benefit of the assessment project has been that the Undergraduate Committee has a way to engage the entire faculty in overall curriculum development goals rather than just dealing with specific issues that arise in specific courses or tracks. The faculty have taken a fresh look at the entire curriculum through the eyes of students enrolled in a set of courses that we think forms a coherent whole, but that the students may not necessarily see that way. By placing the ACEJMC core values and competencies grid over the entire curriculum, the Undergraduate Committee has been able to engage the entire faculty in taking some ownership of the curriculum as a whole rather than simply focusing on a subset of courses or skill sets. If the faculty are going to be held accountable for what students learn as they move through the entire curriculum, then the faculty have to be concerned about that entire set of courses and experiences in a way that they had not been in the past. This has allowed the Undergraduate Committee to enlist the help and advice of virtually everyone on the faculty, as well as a good number of the adjunct instructors, who now have a "stake" in the overall enterprise.

College Leadership

Because the assessment task force sought the advice and help of the CLA Associate Dean for Academic Programs, the SJMC is now positioned as a "leader" in the CLA in implementing larger CLA and U of M goals for student learning assessment as part of the regional accreditation requirements. The CLA is thus enlisted as a partner, and perhaps as a source of support and resources, in implementing the assessment process (which, after all, does not happen without resources). The SJMC benefits by its identity as a forward-thinking entity, by the gratitude of the CLA for taking the first steps in the assessment direction, and by being held up as an example to other CLA units as a way to do assessment "right." For instance, the Associate Dean offered to provide help through the CLA Information Technology Fees Committee staff to adapt the "Portfolio" software to allow for the sampling of student portfolios that our assessment plan outlines.

Challenges in Developing the Assessment Plan

The process of developing a student learning assessment plan has not been without difficulties. For a relatively small faculty charged with delivering a top-notch undergraduate, master's, and PhD-level curriculum, the additional work and effort of reviewing the entire undergraduate curriculum through the assessment lens has proven a monumental undertaking. The Undergraduate Committee has taken the lead, but at the expense of other projects that are equally important and which have usually taken up the bulk of the Committee's efforts in other years. We have yet to feel the full effect of the plan we have proposed, because we have not yet gone through a full cycle of evaluating student work as we have pledged to do. It remains to be seen whether the full implementation of the SJMC's assessment plan is feasible and sustainable.

A much more serious challenge to programs such as the one at the U of M is emerging because of the impending review of communications PhD programs by the National Research Council (NRC). The resources needed to deliver a stellar undergraduate professional program in a liberal arts setting, incorporating all of the work the assessment process demands as a part of accreditation requirements, are substantial. The resources needed to deliver a stellar PhD program in a research university setting, incorporating all of the metrics of the NRC rankings process, also are substantial. In a time of shrinking resources for universities overall, these two sets of demands are on a collision course in programs that strive to do both things well. In the struggle between the undergraduate program accreditation process and the NRC PhD program rankings process, schools or departments housed in major research universities may have to bend to the will of university administrators and presidents who understandably value the NRC rankings much more highly. ACEJMC members need to take this into account in their continuing discussions about the undergraduate accreditation process.

Nonetheless, the process of developing an assessment plan for undergraduate student learning at the U of M has had positive outcomes for students, faculty, and CLA administrators. Students have a clear set of expectations against which they can measure their progress through the major. The faculty have had a chance to review the entire curriculum in light of a well-articulated set of goals for student learning, and have been encouraged to think carefully and creatively about their individual courses and teaching methods. CLA administrators have a model department to point toward as they move the rest of the CLA toward a student learning assessment mind-set for regional accreditation. The process has been a learning opportunity for everyone involved, and that, after all, is the purpose of higher education (for select references, see Appendix D).

Assessment Matrix or Grid Faculty Completed for Each Course Taught

Professional Values and Competencies	Level 1: Awareness (familiarity with specific information, including facts, concepts, laws and regulations, processes and effects)	Level 2: Understanding (assimilation and comprehension of information, concepts, theories and ideas)	Level 3: Application (competence in relating and applying skills, information, concepts, theories and ideas to the accomplishment of tasks)
Understand and apply the principles and laws of freedom of speech and press including the right to dissent, to monitor and criticize power, and to assemble and petition for redress of grievances			
Demonstrate an understanding of the history and role of professionals and institutions in shaping communication			
Demonstrate an understanding of the diversity of groups in a global society in relationship to communications			
Understand concepts and apply theories in the use and presentation of images and information			
Demonstrate an understanding of professional ethical principles and work ethically			
Think critically, creatively and independently			
Conduct research and evaluate information by methods appropriate to the communications profession in which they work			
Write correctly and clearly in forms and styles appropriate for the communications professions, audiences and purposes they serve			
Critically evaluate their own work and that of others for accuracy and fairness, clarity, appropriate style and grammatical correctness			
Apply basic numerical and statistical concepts			
Apply tools and technologies appropriate for the communications professions in which they work			

APPENDIX B

These are examples of two of eight course learning goals for Jour 3004, "Information for Mass Communication." They were developed by Kathleen A. Hansen, School of Journalism and Mass Communication (SJMC) faculty member. These course learning goals are printed on the syllabus and individual course assignments refer to the goal each exercise is addressing. Teaching assistants use the goal and objectives to help in grading assignments. Because this course is required for all SJMC majors, the course learning goals also help faculty teaching the later part of the curriculum to understand what they should expect all students to know as they enter their more advanced courses.

Course Goal: Develop the ability to identify appropriate contributors to an information search	
Action Verb	**Specific Learning Objectives Associated With Course Goal**
Describe	The characteristics of potential contributors to a mass communication information search (informal, institutional, journalistic, scholarly)
Distinguish	Between popular, scholarly and trade sources of information
Identify	Information subsidies and their sources
Distinguish	Between public-sector and private-sector institutions as sources of information

Course Goal: Develop the ability to construct and execute an efficient and effective search for information using print and electronic search tools	
Action Verb	**Specific Learning Objectives Associated With Course Goal**
Categorize	The appropriate tools for a particular search
Plan	An appropriate search strategy (selection of terminology, boundaries of the search, etc.) for the topic
Conduct	A search using appropriate print and electronic tools

APPENDIX C

This is an example of a capstone course project rubric. It was developed by Gayle Golden and Ken Stone, School of Journalism and Mass Communication teaching specialists.

Jour 4451 Advanced Electronic News Writing and Reporting

Objectives	Below expectations	Meets expectations	Above expectations
Research Background Interviews Factual accuracy Context	Lacks context Inappropriate subjects Factual inaccuracies Unfair treatment or one-sidedness	Research provides context Proper camera subjects chosen Fair treatment of issue Facts accurate	*All of "meets expectations" plus:* High complexity of story Added or free points of view add nuance
Use of Video Steadiness and focus Visually interesting shots Proper cutaways Sequencing Lighting	Unsteady camera with bad focusing Poor lighting Boring visual images with little action Lack of cutaways	Camera steady and focused Proper lighting Captured action with interesting camera angle or subject Proper mix of cutaways	*All of "meets expectations" plus:* Lighting enhances story or subject matter Unexpected visuals that complement the script Creative use of cutaways
Use of Sound Capturing ambient sound Using ambient sound for story pace	Little or no ambient sound Ambient sound not integrated with the script	Ambient sound captured Sound used "under" and "up full" for pacing of script	*All of "meets expectations" plus:* Unexpected use of ambient sound that enhances subject
Writing Story structure (lede, foreshadowing, climax) Script relation to video Fairness Factual accuracy Conversational style	Poor story structure missing one element Script at odds with video Presentation of facts confusing Non-conversational style	Strong lede with all story elements Coherent story line Script that complements video Facts woven into story Clear, conversational style	*All of "meets expectations" plus:* Unexpected, effective lede or other story structure element Script that enhances video Facts presented in exceptional way "Elegant" or "poetic" writing touches
Performance (weighted less) Delivery of voice over Use of on-camera standups	False delivery (i.e. sing-song voice, "forced anchor") Stiff body language	Natural delivery Relaxed body language	*All of "meets expectations" plus:* Creative performance details that can include location, camera angle Exceptional eloquence that enhances story

APPENDIX D

Selected Assessment Resources

Angelo, T. A., & Cross, K. P. (1993). *Classroom assessment techniques: A handbook for college teachers* (2nd ed.). San Francisco: Jossey-Bass.

Banta, T. W., Lund, J. P., Black, K. E., & Oblander, F. W. (1996). *Assessment in practice: Putting principles to work on college campuses.* San Francisco: Jossey-Bass.

Gardiner, L., Anderson, C., & Cambridge, B. (1997). *Learning through assessment: A resource guide.* Washington, DC: AAHE.

Glassick, C. E., Huber, M. T., & Maeroff, G. I. (1997). *Scholarship assessed: Evaluation of the professoriate.* San Francisco: Jossey-Bass.

Nichols, J. O. (1995). *A practitioner's handbook for institutional effectiveness and student outcomes assessment implementation* (3rd ed.). New York: Agathon.

Palomba, C. A., & Banta T. W. (Eds.). (2001). *Assessing student competence in accredited disciplines: Pioneering approaches to assessment in higher education.* Herndon, VA: Stylus Publishing, LLC.

Stassen, M. L. A., Doherty, K., & Poe, M. (2001). *Program-based review and assessment: Tools and techniques for program improvement.* Amherst: University of Massachusetts Press.

Walvoord, B. E., & Anderson, V. J. (1998). *Effective grading: A tool for learning and assessment.* San Francisco: Jossey-Bass.

Weimer, M. (2002). *Learner-centered teaching: Five key changes to practice.* San Francisco: Jossey-Bass.

23

Arizona State University

Joe Foote
Gaylord College of Journalism and Mass Communication
University of Oklahoma

Assessment at the Cronkite School of Journalism and Mass Communication at Arizona State University (ASU) began in Spring 2000 when the School created and implemented an assessment plan all in one semester. Because of the severe time constraints, the plan remained very simple and straightforward. This strategy, for the most part, turned out to be a virtue. The School got its assessment vehicle up and running within 3 months and has collected 3 years of data. It is now in the process not only of trying to aggregate and analyze the data it has collected, but also considering a more sophisticated learning outcomes program that will provide more substantive direction for the future of the School.

Largely because of the time constraints for developing a plan, the School did not start with a series of specific learning objectives and then built a learning outcomes system around it. Rather, it started with the broad premises that the School's priorities were training students to compete successfully in the job market after graduation and socializing students into the field by providing them with a background in the ethics, history, societal responsibility, and legal constraints of the field. A key tenet in developing an assessment plan for the School was focusing on both the skills-based competencies and the analytical-based competencies in one plan.

The School's assessment activities are clearly a work in progress. All of the elements described here are seen as "starter measures" that will develop into more precise and comprehensive measures that over time will influence the quality and direction of the program.

The School's assessment plan consists of four basic elements:

1. A senior skills-based assessment of student work at the highest level skills course taken by a student in their chosen concentration (direct measure).
2. A skills-based assessment of individual students' internship experience and their qualifications for the job market (direct measure).
3. A non-skills-based examination covering material covered in the two major required courses (direct measure).
4. Analysis of student satisfaction through an alumni survey conducted by the university (indirect measure).

HIGHER SKILLS ASSESSMENT (DIRECT MEASURE)

A major hurdle for any program is building an effective, direct measure of journalism and mass communication skills. Doing so is a very labor intensive and complex task. Yet, building an assessment plan without one of these direct measures is suspect because so much of a program's reputation lies with its ability to prepare students to be productive members of the workforce. Furthermore, the new assessment standard instituted by the Accrediting Council for Education in Journalism and Mass Communication expects some type of direct measure relating to skills assessment to be incorporated into a quality assessment program.

The gold standard of direct measures of journalism skills assessment is the senior portfolio. Examining the work of students at the end of their university careers provides an important summative snapshot of the effectiveness of their training. The School has taken a few baby steps on its way to a full-fledged senior portfolio assessment. In spring 2000, the School began an external review of a sample of student work in most of its concentrations.

To construct a body of work to measure, the School sampled term projects from the skills classes that were the highest level required of everyone in that concentration. This was somewhat unwieldy because it meant a different assessment in each of five concentrations and the curriculum was changing in some of those concentrations. The faculty decided that an external evaluator and a member of the faculty would jointly review the projects. The evaluation goal was a simple one: Did the work demonstrate a proficiency that would allow that student to enter the workplace in a small media market? Projects were ranked as exemplary, proficient, acceptable, and unacceptable. No precise definitions for each category were provided.

The School paid a small honorarium to the outside evaluators and asked them to come to campus for part of a day to do the evaluations. The concentration heads recruited the outside evaluators from the ranks of media professionals in the state of Arizona. Some heads were particularly vigilant about including small market editors and news directors beyond the metropolitan Phoenix market.

Early on, the administration realized that it would be impractical to examine every student's work so it received permission from the university's assessment coordinator to draw a sample of projects to be examined. The School examined all projects in the smallest concentrations, but drew a sample from the largest.

The simplicity of the project assignment made it relatively easy for outside evaluators to do their work. Having been accustomed to hiring entry-level personnel, they felt confident about rendering a straightforward evaluation that basically came down to the question of "Would you hire this person if you were hiring for a small market?" Unfortunately, the four rankings were not explicitly tied to this general question. What does "proficient" mean compared to "acceptable" in terms of workforce qualifications? How good do you have to be to be judged as "exemplary?" Criteria for each of these rankings need to be created and explained. This is particularly important because the external reviewers frequently rotate through the program.

There were also no explicit directions concerning the split role of the faculty member and the outside evaluator. Were they to rate student work individually without any comparison and take an average? Were they to confer and reach a consensus on the value of the student work? In case of inconsistencies from year to year, did the faculty member have the right to inflate or deflate ratings to maintain a consistent standard?

With 3 years of experience under its belt, the School has learned that it can be difficult to generalize from the data because it can vary so much from concentration to concentration, from reviewer to reviewer, and from year to year. For example, in radio news, the external examiner in 2001 rated two projects exemplary, nine proficient, and two acceptable. A different reviewer in 2002 rated one project exemplary, four proficient, five acceptable, and six unacceptable. A third reviewer in 2003 rated four projects exemplary, six proficient, two acceptable, and none unacceptable. Was there that much change from year to year in the quality of the students' work or did the difference lie in the reviewer? Again, more specific criteria tied to learning objectives and guidance from the faculty evaluator may have mitigated the huge variance in ratings. It is clear that the School will have to make adjustments to how these portfolios are evaluated before it can draw any valid conclusions that can be used to effect program improvement.

In television news, where one news director examined student work for 2 consecutive years, the results were more consistent. In 2002, he rated 1 project exemplary, 6 proficient, 16 acceptable, and 8 unacceptable. The following year he rated none exemplary, 5 proficient, 21 acceptable, and 9 unacceptable. Although there was a different reviewer in 2001, the results were still consistent: none exemplary, two proficient, nine acceptable, and seven unacceptable.

Overall, there were some stark discrepancies across sequences. Only 5% of the projects from public relations (PR) and news editorial were judged as "unacceptable" over the 3-year period, whereas 15% of the radio news projects and 29% of the television news were judged as unacceptable. Why were TV news students failing six times more often than their PR and print counterparts? Why were 86% of the failures in the broadcast news area?

Similarly, more than one third of the news editorial rankings were in the exemplary range compared to only 1% in television, creating another conundrum for the faculty. At some point, the faculty and administration will have to come to grips with these discrepancies and ascertain whether the results are an artifact of the assessment process or a real indicator of quality in the program? And, how is an administrator to reconcile this? On the one hand, broadcast students won first place nationally in the Hearst writing competition in 2003 to 2004, whereas the print students did not finish in the top 10. Yet, the assessment results showed that far more print students were judged exemplary than broadcast students.

If some of the results are suspect, what can be gained from this type of analysis? The broad assessment of School students showed that over 3 years, 83% of its graduates were rated in the "acceptable" or higher range to assume an entry-level job in the industry. It now has a 3-year benchmark on which to build. If it can make the evaluation more consistent and better define criteria, the value of this measure will certainly improve.

A major disadvantage of this crude measure was that it offered little insight into the elements that might have produced a highly qualified graduate. Although we did learn that a high proportion of our graduates were deemed ready for the job market, we did not learn what value-added part of their university education got them there? When the School enters the next phase of its assessment experience, it is likely to refine these measures, teasing out some of the individual components of a quality journalism and mass communication education. Some of the outside evaluators explained why certain elements of the projects appealed to them and what areas were strongest, but there were no predefined parameters for this kind of feedback.

Even the implementation of the external skills assessment revealed some flaws in our execution of the curriculum. Two different professors taught broadcast management, the highest level course in the media management concentration. One professor required a reality-based group project that required considerable knowledge of the local television marketplace to complete. The other did not. The two professors were reluctant to conform their courses to a common syllabus so the skills assessment was postponed in this concentration until the differences could be reconciled. Three years later, there is still no evaluative measure.

This part of the assessment debate prompted cries of "academic freedom" from other faculty who were reluctant to conform their section of a multiple section course to a common syllabus. In my mind, this is symptomatic of a singular lack of emphasis on quality control in higher education. The notion of the independent professor going his or her own way with minimum interference has ruled since journalism has been taught at the university level. Because journalism education has historically not been a player in the general education curriculum, conflicts over multiple section consistency seldom arise. With assessment, however, quality control takes priority. Students, parents, and education stakeholders expect that an education has a significant degree of internal consistency across sections and professors. Once assessment measures become more refined and focused, the wisdom of this demand should become evident.

Although the School's summative skills evaluation was one-dimensional, it was an important and productive first step toward a deeper form of direct measurement. One of the most important outcomes of this exercise has been the routinization of the assessment process. It has put the School into a rhythm of examining the skill level of its students. There is now an expectation that student work will be evaluated beyond the classroom based on criteria that transcend course grades. The faculty anxiety that initially accompanied this activity has largely disappeared. The exercise has laid an excellent foundation for a segue into a full-blown portfolio review.

The external review has reassured the faculty that it is doing a competent job of instruction and that the great majority of students are ready to assume a productive role in the workplace. A full-fledged portfolio review will further expose students' full range of abilities within and across media, their ability to package their work persuasively, and their creativity beyond the narrowness of prescribed assignments.

I would hope that the second-generation assessment of skills would examine breadth as well as depth in the curriculum. In addition to their focused goal of preparing for a particular job in a particular medium, can students demonstrate other skills as well? Do they possess skills beyond their narrowly defined concentration? Do they have the ability to integrate different forms of media in a productive way? Do they exhibit any higher level characteristics that go beyond their ability to get a first job?

It would also be helpful to have a coordinated measure that invites comparison across concentrations. Historically, there has been a chauvinism in journalism schools that blatantly discriminates against certain areas of study, implying that they are lightweight inferiors in terms of skills and sophistication. Developing a common denominator of quality would provide a more objective assessment to compare students throughout the major. Having an externally validated measure of writing is another need for a direct measure in journalism. Projects that are evaluated on their creativity, their writing quality, and their visual quality (when appropriate) would help programs understand better the kinds of graduates they are producing.

INTERNSHIP ASSESSMENT (DIRECT MEASURE)

One of the most overlooked assessment measures is evaluation of the student internship (see chapter 17). These can be direct or indirect, depending on how the data are collected and used. Many programs already collect enough data to do a broad assessment of the program and most programs could do so with minimal effort. Some might ask, what is the difference between giving course grades for internships and using internships for evaluating learning outcomes? The data gathered may not be much different, but the ways in which the data are used are significantly different. When employers rate a student intern, they are in a position to rate directly the competence of the student and their prospects in the marketplace. Thus, the rating of individual students' professional performance in a systematic way provides a valuable, direct measure of assessment. A more general evaluation that is not tied to assessment of students as individuals would be an indirect measure.

Grades for internships reflect the individual achievement of a particular student for a given internship as rated by the instructor of record. The input of employer supervisors provides a valid external evaluation that offers a second perspective to an instructor's evaluation and can be aggregated across that supervisors' total experience with interns. Furthermore, all of the employer supervisors' collective input can be used to provide not only a measure of the internships' cumulative worth, but also the skills preparation of several generations of interns.

The internship evaluation is an excellent complement to the senior portfolio because they are both examining the skill level of students. There should be a high correlation between the external review of senior portfolios and the cumulative assessment of the skills exhibited during internships. One has to control, however, for the different population entering internships if a select group is chosen for the internship experience.

If the right questions are asked, the internship assessment can also provide an external measure of the students' work ethic, their integration into a workplace, their problem-solving ability, and their knowledge beyond journalism, including their broad-based liberal arts education. The first incarnation of the ASU internship assessment effort did not delve into these subsidiary areas, but focused instead on the central questions of "If there were an opening for an entry-level position at your company, would you hire this person?" and "Is this student ready for an entry-level job in a small market?" With the evaluation conducted in a top-20 market, students fared far better on the suitability for entry-level employment than they did on the readiness to work for a major market station. Yet, a sizable percentage was deemed ready for that higher level opportunity.

As with the skills project assessment, the internship assessment results revealed several inconsistencies. Over the 3-year period, 91% of School students were judged by their employers to be ready to enter the marketplace, a great tribute to the quality of the program. Yet, the failure rate among broadcast journalism students was far higher than with other concentrations. Ninety percent of the failures were in the broadcast area. Conversely, no PR and sales interns and only two of the news editorial interns were deemed unready for the workplace, casting doubts on the validity of the measure.

The next iteration of internship assessment provides an opportunity to make midcourse corrections to counter these inconsistencies and delve deeper into the qualities that quality interns possess. A great deal of feedback from employer supervisors relates to the students' intangible personal qualities and their ability to work with others. And, if students do have a very narrow view of the world that limits their potential, it will normally become manifest in an internship.

It would be nice if these factors could be incorporated into the assessment process. A challenge is to gather as much information as possible without creating an onerous burden for the employer supervisor. The School has wisely kept its evaluation very simple and straightforward. The best system is one that seamlessly gathers data necessary for evaluating the student in the internship and the program effectiveness overall with the same prompts. One would hope that these data could be used more creatively to use the internship as a direct measure of the skills training of the program and the liberal arts knowledge that students typically exhibit.

COMPREHENSIVE EXAM (DIRECT MEASURE)

In addition to skills assessment, the faculty wanted to learn more about the competencies the students were developing in two core courses required of each student in the major (Media and Society, and Law of Mass Communication). Because all students take these courses, the School decided to administer an exam in the law class each semester that measured some of the content covered in the courses. One of the law instructors constructed an exam of 20 objective questions using basic content from the two required courses and began administering it in all of the law sections in 2001.

The questions on the exam were very basic, mostly involving the structure of media and the rudiments of libel and privacy. The questions were not explicitly tied to particular, established learning outcomes.

Three years of data show consistent results. Students scored 77%, 75%, and 78% over the 3 years. No level was set for a satisfactory result, and results were not broken down according to percentiles. Clearly, there is proficiency in the areas tested among a majority of students based on the content of the exam. What the School has not done is tie the questions on the test to specific competencies. We know that most Cronkite students leave with a passing score on this exam, but little else. We do not have any additional knowledge about particular areas where they are weak or strong.

An opportunity now exists to expand the exam with a discreet section devoted to a particular competency. There is also an opportunity to give a pretest at the beginning of the Media and Society class that students take during their freshman or sophomore years that can be compared to the summative exam taken during their senior year in the law course.

STUDENT SATISFACTION SURVEY (INDIRECT MEASURE)

One of the easiest and most useful indirect measures of assessment has proven to be surveys of recent graduates by the university. Most universities have had considerable experience with this instrument and have refined it over the years to be a valuable tool. For the units using this measure, finding feedback to help the program has been relatively simple. Also, it is the most useful tool to feed back into the system to effect change. Most programs are able to use these data to make immediate improvements unlike some other assessment tools that take years to unfold.

Most recent graduate surveys ask about student satisfaction with such things as advising, job placement, orientation, internships, obtaining classes, and so forth. They also ask about how well the program prepared students in writing, oral presentations, and technology usage, as well as their overall level of satisfaction. Results are usually broken out across colleges and departments, gender, ethnicity, in-state–out-of-state, and age.

The recent graduate survey at Arizona State spoke clearly about strengths and weaknesses. For several years, the School's professional advising system in which a student kept the same advisor from matriculation to graduation received overwhelming validation. Students clearly understood the value of this personalized, consistent advising.

The major weakness also appeared across several groups of graduates—career placement. The School had relied on an informal system of career placement tied to its extremely well developed internship program. Job notices were posted informally with the School and advice was dispensed through faculty, sequence heads and internship coordinators. No faculty or staff member was specifically charged with coordinating career advice and services. There was little coordination between the university's career placement center and the School's efforts. Students who participated in the internship program (not required of all students) had much higher satisfaction than those who did not. Thus, students without an internship or other work experience on their resume felt cut off from any real help in the marketplace for employment.

Seeing graduates' consistent negative feedback in the alumni survey on job placement, the School began to change its strategy. First, it forged a much closer link with the university's career placement service. It stopped posting its own job notices and started funneling them directly to career placement. Advisors began steering students to career placement and encouraged career placement to be more proactive in inviting national media recruiters to campus. Internship coordinators started using career placement's facilities to hold interviews to expose students to their location and services.

The School tried to convince students that career placement's database, which provided opportunities for employers to search out students as well as students searching for employers, was a huge advantage in the marketplace. It was clear, however, that this partnership was not sufficient to give students the kind of localized career advice they required. Recently, the School's Director added a career counselor as a budget priority. This person, when hired, would serve as a liaison between career services, the internship coordinators, and the School, to improve the service students receive and would initiate a series of interviewing, resume writing, and career preparation workshops for students.

In addition to these two areas where the results were striking, there were other categories that validated conventional wisdom. As expected, students felt that they had received abundant experience in writing, had been given great opportunity for hands-on training, and had developed a close relationship with the faculty. Yet, it was surprising that these journalism students, who had been nurtured in small classes for most of their tenure in the School and had developed a relationship with the faculty, were not significantly more satisfied than students in most other units in the campus, including some that offered a far more impersonal atmosphere and experience. Particularly surprising was a positive response to the writing experience question from students in a department where minimal writing experience was offered. It seemed that students could be socialized into thinking that they were getting a significant amount of experience although it did not square with reality. It shows the relative isolation of individual majors and the inability of students to compare experiences outside of that cocoon.

One mistake that many departments make with senior and recent graduate surveys is looking at their own data exclusively and not comparing them to other units and the university as a whole. These surveys are one of the few assessment measures where upper level administrators can make comparisons across units. It is helpful for a journalism and mass communication department to build a solid case for the unit based on its consistent showing in these surveys. Likewise, a unit can gauge its own status within the university across a variety of measures. It is important to examine several years of data to get a realistic view of our graduates' perceptions. Yet, it is remarkable how consistent they are from year to year.

Before putting too much stock in an alumni survey, assessment coordinators should keep in mind that that the return rate on these surveys is usually low, lowering the probability that they are representative of the entire population. They rely on the recollections of alumni, which may or may not be distorted. Also, their recommendations may be dated if the curriculum or student services have changed since their time at the university.

Although the new graduates survey has been a productive measure for the School and has been used to make adjustments in the program, it is not officially part of the School's assessment plan. Sometimes departments don't realize that the mounds of data collected by the university can be an important part of their local assessment activities (see chapter 16). It would be wise for a departmental assessment coordinator to examine the full range of university data from university surveys to see what parts might be useful for journalism and mass communication assessment.

OTHER POTENTIAL ASSESSMENT AREAS (INDIRECT MEASURES)

One indirect measurement of quality that the School is already using on an informal basis is the regional and national recognition that students receive. The School is very active in the Hearst, Society of Professional Journalists, Broadcast Education, and Roy Howard awards, winning numerous prizes. The analysis of these honors over time would show a consistency of quality that routinely produces high achievers. Although this is not a measure of the quality of the entire student body, it demonstrates the ability to draw highly talented students to the program consistently and to help them achieve a level of competence that rates with the best in the nation.

RECOMMENDATIONS

In the first 3 years of its outcomes assessment experience, the School has shown that it can marshal the resources to sustain an ongoing assessment plan that features both direct and indirect measures. It has also demonstrated that it can attract a panel of respected external reviewers who are pleased to work with faculty to evaluate the program.

Armed with this initial experience, the School is ready to consider refinements and improvements. To that end, I would make the following recommendations. First, the School should make the graduate survey an official part of its assessment program. Doing so would establish a focused database for student feedback. Because the School is already using many of the results, the effort to include this measure officially would be minimal. Special attention should be paid to comparing results with those of other departments on campus.

Second, the School should expand the project evaluation in the highest skills class into a full-fledged senior portfolio evaluation. The multiple projects from five different classes have become unwieldy, and it is difficult to bring consistency across reviewers to the evaluation. A portfolio assessment would allow the student greater flexibility and creativity. The School would be able to have individual judges evaluate students across concentrations, mitigating the differences between broadcast journalism and the rest of the curriculum. Perfecting this measure should be the prime focus of any journalism program's assessment plan because it goes to the heart of professional education and a student's readiness to enter the workplace.

Third, better definition should be given to the grading scale for evaluating projects so that there can be better consistency across reviewers, across years, and between concentrations. This exposes the gap between constructing an assessment plan and executing one that provides meaningful feedback for change. Unless the measurement system is precise and consistent and tied to specific outcomes, the results can be a jumble of unusable information.

Fourth, competencies should be established for the summative project beyond the ability of the student to compete in the workplace. Individual measures of writing, organization, and analytical skills could be assessed. Although preparing a student for the workplace is an important dimension of a quality journalism education, it is not the only dimension. The portfolio should go farther than ascertaining the ability of a graduate to find a job.

Fifth, the criteria for the internship evaluation should be refined to give a more robust evaluation of the internship experience and to increase the reliability of evaluators over time and across concentrations. In its current state, the School is processing the minimum amount of information from internships to assess skills. A more detailed evaluation could gauge the writing and presentational skills of the students and their liberal arts knowledge over time. It would also be helpful if the project evaluation and the internship measurements could be interrelated to provide a stronger and more robust measurement of journalism and mass communication skills.

Sixth, specific learning competencies should be established for the comprehensive exam to deliver specific information about strengths and weaknesses of specific areas rather than a general score on a test and nothing else. It is of little use to know that a certain percentage of students can pass an exam. What is needed is evidence tied to individual learning competencies so the faculty can see over time where strengths and weaknesses of the program lie. This would require more comprehensive exam on law, ethics, history, and media structure, and a much more detailed analysis. Furthermore, the testing process should be expanded to include a pretest in the freshman class as well as a summative exam in the law class to provide a better baseline of the knowledge of entering students. A program needs to know not only where the students stand when they graduate, but the kinds of knowledge they brought to the program.

Seventh, the School should incorporate its analysis of regional and national awards contests in which Cronkite students compete into the assessment process. Although this indirect measure would gauge the quality of elite students only, it would be a valuable secondary measure to complement some of the direct measures. Because most schools compete in national contents, a longitudinal analysis of their performance could be valuable in gauging quality.

Eighth, the School should begin to aggregate data across years and across concentrations rather than reporting results only in a single year as is being done now. To really benefit from assessment and effect change, programs must think about data over time. It is only when one measures competencies and attitudes over several years that programs can ascertain strengths and weaknesses and move in a new direction with confidence. In fact, it is quite exciting to see trends develop and make decisions based on empirical evidence. One of the chief measures of maturation in an assessment plan is how it makes the transition from taking isolated snapshots to using an accumulation of those snapshots to get a broader and deeper picture.

COMPLETING THE LOOP

The assessment program in the School, like with most other programs, began as a process to achieve a requirement. It was not begun because the School wanted to test a particular hypothesis or answer a burning curricular question. Success was often seen as having evaluation measures that met the test of central administration and executing the evaluation on schedule. Outcomes sought seemed to be the validation of quality rather than the discovery of new information that might result in improvements. My experience has been that such a defensive position is quite natural and has to work its way through the system. Therefore, I see it as entirely functional to have a shakedown cruise in the mechanics of evaluation before getting down to the business of true discovery. Once the fear of assessment and its associated misconceptions fade, attention can turn to solving real problems.

Let me relate a few issues being debated in the School where assessment could enlighten the debate. For the past 4 years, the Cronkite faculty, like many others around the country, have been debating the value of convergence in the undergraduate curriculum. Frequently, the assertion is made that sacrificing depth for breadth could have negative consequences for students in the workplace. Are there significant differences in outcomes from curricula based on two different philosophies? Are students from a converged curriculum less able to compete in the workplace than from a single-medium curriculum? We will keep debating based on anecdotal evidence until someone can measure how capable graduates are from each type of program.

A collateral issue concerns the two writing classes required of all journalism students. They are basically two print courses, newswriting and reporting. A recurring question has been the effect that having all journalism students takes these courses will have. Print students are not getting the cross-platform experience that broadcast students are receiving. Is this hurting the print students' ability to compete? Is requiring broadcast students to take two print courses strengthening their writing skills and making them more marketable? Are they losing the opportunity to gain additional broadcast journalism skills in the process?

There is also the ongoing debate between professionals and journalism educators about whether journalism students are developing sufficient writing skills. This debate will run endlessly in circles until outcomes assessment reaches maturity where the question can be settled based on hard data.

The faculty is debating whether there should be a standalone ethics course or it should continue to integrate ethics into several courses. Are they currently doing enough ethics instruction? Is the integrated approach working? An expanded senior exam could help answer these questions by showing the ethics knowledge that students now have when they graduate. If a competency were already being achieved, there would be little need to create a new required course.

A new concentration, Media Analysis and Criticism, has become suspect. Several journalism faculty members have questioned what students actually learn in that concentration, whether students are employable, and whether it is as rigorous as the other concentrations. We will never know the answers unless we measure the specific outcomes in that concentration.

In a curricular revision 3 years ago, PR students were no longer required to take the reporting class. Several journalism faculty members contended that this would have adverse results on the PR students' readiness. It would have been nice to have a comprehensive assessment package in place so we could have actually measured the differences in skill levels before and after the change. Still, we could pay particular attention to the writing scores on senior portfolios to assess if PR students have sufficient writing training to be successful in their careers.

There is a debate currently over whether the production concentration, resurrected 3 years ago, should be retired once again. One of the contentions is that the concentration produces only "button pushers" and does not require the same creative standards as other concentrations. Direct measures of skills such as a senior portfolio could ascertain whether graduating students are expressing themselves creatively or just learning to use technology.

These are just a few issues that outcomes assessment could enlighten. True success will come when faculties and administrators sincerely seek answers to these kinds of problems. In the meantime, the School is slowly building the infrastructure that will allow this more mature phase to unfold.

APPENDIX

Cronkite School: Learning Outcome Assessment Program

Goals/Learning Outcomes

The primary mission of the Cronkite School is to prepare students to enter positions in media fields.

Graduates of the Cronkite School are expected to demonstrate skills in writing, reporting, editing and production while acquiring a basic knowledge of media businesses and operations. They also are expected to have a basic knowledge of mass communication law and ethics.

Students are expected to be prepared to assume an entry-level position in a professional media outlet upon graduation from the Cronkite School.

Learning assessment is designed to determine outcomes for the area concentrations in the Cronkite School.

Methodology

It was determined by the faculty that learning outcomes assessment should be conducted according to three strategies:

1. All students in the highest level class required of all Cronkite School majors, Mass Communication Law, will be given a set of 20 relevant questions constructed by the faculty who teach the course. The questions are designed to measure a basic level of knowledge of media law, ethics and history. The questions are objective and student responses were analyzed by computer following administration of the exam. As-

sessment criteria are the percentage of correct responses for each student and the mean score for all students.

2. A sample (50%) of student projects from the highest level courses in each concentration that every student in that concentration must take will be assessed. The sample should include projects from fall and spring semesters. The projects are then evaluated by media professionals in cooperation with a Cronkite School faculty member. The reviewers are asked to determine whether the student projects reflect a skill level necessary to obtain an entry-level position in, at least, a small market (defined as Arbitron 101-plus market size for broadcast stations or circulation 5,000 or less for newspapers). Project evaluation is quantified according to the scoring hierarchy: exemplary, proficient, acceptable and unacceptable. Each year, the news-editorial, broadcast journalism and public relations concentrations are assessed. Student projects from Reporting Public Affairs, Broadcast News Reporting, Advanced Broadcast Reporting and Public Relations Campaigns are evaluated. Students graduating from the new, converged curriculum will submit portfolios representing their work in Journalism, Media Analysis & Criticism, Media Management, Media Production or Strategic Media & Public Relations for evaluation.

3. Professional program student internships are assessed to determine preparation level for an entry-level position. Intern agency coordinators are asked if, based on their evaluation of the student intern, they would hire the student if an entry-level were available. The responses are used to determine if the student was prepared at an adequate level to assume an entry-level media position.

Walter Cronkite School of Journalism and Mass Communication. "Learning Outcome Assessment Program." Arizona State University, 2001.

TABLE 23.1
Cronkite School Assessment Summary

Competency/Outcome	Measurement Tools	Type of Measure	Feedback Outcomes
Highest-level Skills Assessment	Portfolio	Direct	Outcomes pending
Professional Readiness Measure	Employer assessment of student interns	Direct	Outcomes pending
Knowledge-based Outcome	Senior examination	Direct	Outcomes pending
Student Satisfaction	Alumni Survey	Indirect	Priority on career services for students; validation of advising system

24

Virginia Commonwealth University

Paula Otto
Jean M. Yerian
Judy VanSlyke Turk
Virginia Commonwealth University

Located on two downtown campuses in Richmond, VA, and with a campus in Doha, Qatar, Virginia Commonwealth University (VCU) is ranked nationally by the Carnegie Foundation as a top research institution. VCU enrolls more than 26,000 students in over 170 certificate, undergraduate, graduate, professional, and doctoral programs in the arts, sciences, humanities, and health professions, in 11 schools and 1 college.

Forty of the university's programs are unique in Virginia, and *U.S. News & World Report* ranked 20 of VCU's graduate and professional programs as among the best of their kind. Medical College of Virginia Campus hospitals, clinics, and the health sciences schools of VCU compose the VCU Medical Center, the fourth largest academic medical center in the country.

The School of Mass Communications (School) is one of the largest programs in VCU's College of Humanities and Sciences, with a growing enrollment of more than 900 undergraduate students and 120 students at the Adcenter, the School's graduate program in advertising. The School offers three sequences of specialized study at the undergraduate level: Advertising (with a concentration in creative or business), Journalism (with a concentration in print or broadcasting), and Public Relations.

Formed by a merger of the Medical College of Virginia and Richmond Professional Institute in 1968, VCU has a strong tradition of decentralization. Throughout most of its history, VCU has left the assessment of student learning outcomes in the hands (and files) of academic schools and departments.

A NEW VIEW ON ACCOUNTABILITY AND ASSESSMENT

However, recent changes in public emphasis on and scrutiny of quality assurance and enhancement in higher education made it clear that the university has a compelling interest in developing additional structure for assessment. In fact, the interest in accountability is now readily apparent both externally and internally: VCU has over 90 academic programs with specific disciplinary accreditations; the State Council of Higher Education for Virginia (SCHEV) requires public institutions to report on general education core competencies; and VCU's own Strategic Plan specifies a comprehensive program review process.

Another major driver for VCU's increase in assessment structure was an approaching reaffirmation-of-accreditation review by the Southern Association of Colleges and Schools (SACS). Like most regional accreditors, SACS asks its members to present proof of their "institutional effectiveness" (Commission on Colleges of the Southern Association of Colleges and Schools, 2004, p. 22): "The institution *identifies expected outcomes* for its educational programs and its administrative and educational support services; *assesses whether it achieves these outcomes*; and *provides evidence of improvement* based on analysis of those results" (italics added for emphasis).

VCU'S OWN ASSESSMENT TOOL

VCU is committed to developing its own system, which could be used by academic programs as well as administrative and educational support services to both "prove" (summative assessment) and "improve" (formative assessment) teaching and learning. The original development team members were from Institutional Research and Evaluation and Academic Technology, although development later included representatives from Academic Affairs, eventually being led by the university's new Director of Assessment.

The team adopted the name WEAVE for VCU's approach, an acronym for an assessment cycle in which all VCU units—academic programs and administrative and educational support services alike—would

- **W**rite expected outcomes and objectives.
- **E**stablish criteria for success.
- **A**ssess performance against criteria.
- **V**iew assessment results.
- **E**ffect improvements through actions.

In its first iteration, WEAVE was a fairly linear database. On something called a Quality Enhancement Reporting Form, an academic program specified its mission, then identified learning outcomes. Each student learning outcome (or other outcome or objective, depending on the mission) was tracked through the entire assessment process. First, the academic program stated the outcome; the program could also show the outcome's relation to general education requirements. Next, the program stated any assessment activities (measures) that would be used to assess the outcome and gave both criteria for success and time-tables for those measures. Later on, the program entered actual assessment findings and "use of assessment results."

WEAVE had several problems. For example, if an academic program used the same measure—such as a portfolio or a comprehensive exam—to assess several outcomes, WEAVE required separate entry of that measure under each individual outcome. Similarly, a program might decide to plan an action (use of results) after seeing problematic findings from several different measures; because an action would have to be entered separately for each measure, the linear nature of WEAVE led to duplicate work for users. As a result of what were called assessment assemblies on both Richmond campuses, the development team reached out to all faculty and staff users and then took their feedback to make dramatic changes.

WEAVEonline™ was introduced at VCU in March 2003. (The next version of *WEAVEonline*™, which also will be available as a hosted subscription service outside VCU, is scheduled for release in 2005.) It is an innovative Web-based assessment management system, which is a transformational addition to VCU's toolbox. For the first time, VCU has a way to automate the capture and analysis of information to support continuing improvement efforts in individual programs and services throughout the university. The application's easy-to-use interface organizes data by each unit's mission, objectives and outcomes, assessment measures and findings, planned actions to effect future improvements to programs and services, and reflective analyses. There are also built-in planning, reporting, tracking, and feedback features.

Currently, *WEAVEonline*™ automates university processes to

- Document assessment of student learning outcomes in academic programs.
- Document assessment of outcomes and objectives in administrative and educational support programs.
- Provide data needed for reports to state higher education bodies and to regional and other accrediting agencies.

- Support university program review—both academic and administrative or educational support programs.
- Provide status information on various university-wide initiatives and elements of the strategic plan.
- Provide information for annual reporting purposes.

This centralized pool of data on program intentions and performance allows vertical integration of quality improvement from the unit level through to school or college level and beyond and facilitates accreditation, program reviews, and annual reporting. Built into *WEAVEonline*™ is the automated cross-unit consolidation of information, for example, aggregation of data for all units supporting a specific general education requirement.

WEAVEonline™ both leads and supports the assessment process. Here are the questions an academic program must answer in developing its *WEAVEonline*™ entries:

- What is the academic program's core mission?
- What are the program's critical student learning outcomes?
- How do these student learning outcomes relate to the larger educational context, such as general educational competencies? (*WEAVEonline*™ also allows programs to make other associations, such as relation to any disciplinary accreditation standards.)
- What measures can the program use to monitor student performance on the outcomes? (There should be direct measures of student learning, e.g., rating of a student's news stories by a panel of faculty and local editors. There also can be indirect measures, e.g., graduates' ratings of their perceived skill development as a result of the program.)
- What "target level" of performance on each of those measures is acceptable to the program?
- How do actual results of the assessments compare with the target levels set?
- What strengths has the program affirmed through assessment?
- What assessed areas require future attention?
- If action is indicated to improve performance to acceptable levels, what action will the program take?

Academic and support programs can run self-audits in *WEAVEonline*™ to make sure their entries are complete, for example, findings are reported for all measures. Programs can export basic data to Microsoft Excel. Incorporated into the application is a detailed assessment report, which shows all associations in full and can be exported to Microsoft Word. There also is an assessment summary report that can be run at unit (program), division (school or college), and university levels.

WEAVEonline™ can record feedback on its assessment processes as well as responses to the feedback. Through a central system interface, the director of assessment can help academic and support programs identify who else at VCU is using a particular assessment approach, such as portfolios. This enables communities of practice to emerge and faculty-staff to enhance their practice by collaborating with local peers.

WEAVEonline™ is an application that fits VCU's culture. It establishes a template to ask a basic effectiveness question: "Are your efforts bringing forth the desired results?" (FranklinCovey Co., 2003). There is a sense of pride at the university about its excellent programs and services. Now there is a repository for the good news of how well the university is doing in most areas and a benchmarking process for discerning those areas that are candidates for further improvement.

The Higher Learning Commission (HLC), a Commission of the North Central Association of Colleges and Schools (NCA), another regional accreditor, published "An Assessment Culture Matrix" (2003) identifying a number of elements that would indicate an institution's "Maturing Stages of Continuous Improvement" in assessment of student academic achievement. The structure of *WEAVEonline*™ clearly addresses several key elements in "An Assessment Culture Matrix":

> The assessment program materials developed at the institutional level reflect the emphasis of the Mission and Purposes statements on the importance of identifying learning expectations, on determining the outcomes of assessing student learning across academic programs, and on using assessment results to improve student learning. (HLC/NCA, 2003, p. 72)

> The institution maintains a system of data collection that helps sustain an effective assessment program. (HLC/NCA, 2003, p. 77)

> Programmatic benchmarks are established against which students' learning outcomes are assessed. (HLC/NCA, 2003, p. 79)

The School of Mass Communications

As the undergraduate programs in VCU's School began to develop their outcome-based measures, the faculty had four goals:

- To fulfill the university's requirements.
- To incorporate goals outlined in the School's strategic plan.

- To incorporate findings from a 1997 survey of newsroom management regarding the skills students need to succeed in the communications industry.
- To incorporate the guidelines of the Accrediting Council on Education in Journalism and Mass Communications (ACEJMC).

At the same time that the university was requiring all of its units to participate in the WEAVE process described earlier, the School was preparing to undergo a major study of its curriculum and was entering the first stage of preparation for the ACEJMC accreditation process.

Because the School's permanent full-time faculty is relatively small (15), they worked on the project as a committee of the whole, with leadership from the School's director and assistant director. The School at that time had four possible curriculum sequences: advertising, broadcast journalism, print journalism, and public relations. After a significant curriculum revamping in the 2002 to 2003 academic year, the two journalism tracks were combined into one.

Guiding Principles in Developing the Assessment Plan

The School's Strategic Plan. The School's strategic plan outlines the following vision: It is the vision of the School of Mass Communications to develop a community of learning in which

- The curriculum is responsive to the rapidly changing fields of communication.
- Students and faculty collaborate to explore and master new media technologies, including digital and interactive.
- Students are prepared to produce and disseminate information in multiple formats, including written text, audio, video and the Web.

The strategic plan further outlines curriculum goals with several accompanying strategies.

Goal: The School of Mass Communications Will Deliver a Curriculum That Gives Students a Solid Foundation in Both the Theory and Practice of Journalism, Advertising, Public Relations, and Developing Media.

- Strategy: The School will implement the new undergraduate curriculum approved at the end of the 2002 to 2003 academic year.
- Strategy: The School will infuse students into the workplace through internships and other real-world experiences.

- Strategy: The curriculum will be under constant review to ensure that it keeps pace with and emphasizes "best practices" in the rapidly changing fields of communication, including but not limited to technological advances and philosophical shifts.

Goal: The School's Curriculum Will Foster Collaborative Learning, With Students Learning From Each Other, From Experts in the Professions, and From Faculty.

- Strategy: Faculty members will be encouraged to maintain "state of the art" expertise that is comparable to industry practices and expectations.
- Strategy: The School will implement the merger of the Electronic Media and News-Editorial programs into one Journalism sequence and will implement the courses that provide students with the opportunity for cross-platform and collaborative learning.
- Strategy: The School will encourage creation of opportunities for advertising and public relations majors to practice the integration of various communication tactics and techniques.
- Strategy: The curriculum will provide opportunities for students and faculty to collaborate to explore and master new technologies, including digital and interactive media.

Survey of News Managers

A 1997 nationwide survey of news managers conducted for the VCU School and the Associated Press Managing Editors by Ketchum Public Relations found the following:

- News managers believe writing is the most important skill for undergraduate journalism students to have.
- Reporting, ethics and interviewing skills are very important in the undergraduate curriculum.
- It is extremely important for journalists—and those who work in related fields such as advertising and public relations—to effectively incorporate creative thinking and analysis.
- Internship programs are extremely important.

ACEJMC STANDARDS OF ACCREDITATION

These reflect the newly revised standards, effective in the 2004 to 2005 academic year. The ACEJMC was in the process of revising the standards when the School was writing its strategic plan and assessment objectives. The School used early drafts of the new standards, as well as the existing standards, to develop its objectives. See the ACEJMC's (2004) *Journalism and Mass Communications Accreditation (2004–2005)* for a complete list of the final standards and the core values and competencies.

The two ACEJMC standards that faculty used in developing the School's assessment plan were Standard 2, Curriculum and Instruction and Standard 9. Assessment is expected to provide a curriculum and instruction that enables students to learn the knowledge, competencies and values the Council defines for preparing students to work in a diverse global and domestic society. The unit, based on requirements of Standard 9, regularly assesses student learning and uses results to improve curriculum and instruction.

Writing the School's Assessment Goals

Using the School's strategic plan, the newsroom management survey results, and the ACEJMC guidelines, the faculty first outlined three overarching objectives and nine core skill and competency measurement areas for all majors. This also followed the University's WEAVE matrix.

Objectives

Graduates of the School should be able to

1. Communicate clearly and effectively in forms and styles appropriate for the communications professions, audiences, and purposes they serve.
2. Understand a core of fundamental concepts, values, and skills that include strategy development, critical thinking, problem solving, and understanding the ethical and legal implications of the media and communication industries.
3. Apply tools and technologies appropriate for the communications profession in which they work.

Nine measures were identified for these objectives:

1. Entrance testing for *Writing for the Media* course (covers grammar, punctuation, and spelling proficiency).
2. Rating of numerous writing examples during the *Writing for the Media* course to demonstrate that students understand how to organize and present information in appropriate, correct news style, and that their writing is of substantial quality.

3. Communication skills assessment by faculty and professionals, done in capstone courses.

4. Internship evaluation of student on professional communication tasks, done by intern supervisors and faculty.

5. Rating of student's ability to demonstrate successful problem solving, critical thinking, and strategic planning and execution, as well ability to use channels of mass communications in a responsible and ethical manner by faculty and professionals in capstone courses.

6. Through questions on a final exam in the Mass Media Ethics course, rating student ability to think critically, analyze ethical dilemmas, and solve ethical problems.

7. Through questions on a final exam in the Mass Media Law course, rating student understanding of the role media play in society, and the importance of First Amendment rights in a democratic society.

8. Through College of Humanities and Sciences SmartForce testing, assessing students' basic computer competency in word processing, file management, and Internet use.

9. Rating of student's basic competency in the technology skills needed in each specialty—advertising, public relations, print journalism, and broadcast journalism—made by faculty using a scoring rubric or checklist.

Table 24.1 summarizes the objectives and measures. Whenever possible, the faculty did not use test results as a measure. However, in some cases, such as the senior-level law course which often has 50+ students, a final exam is the most practical measurement tool. Test questions are also used to measure objectives in the sophomore-level ethics course. Although not reflected in the formal measures, ethics continues to be tested informally as students progress through the curriculum and encounter ethical issues and dilemmas in producing stories and other communications materials.

Once the measures were developed, the next step was for faculty to develop expected performance levels to create a standard against which achievement could be measured and assessed. For the first year, the faculty determined appropriate levels of success (e.g., 55% passing level) based on their experience of past student performance. The first measurement cycle was the 2002 to 2003 academic year. Measures were generally administered by faculty, except where noted that outside professionals were used, such as in judging capstone coursework projects.

Although some may question the use of faculty assessing their own students as too similar to using course grades as a measurement, the

TABLE 24.1
Objectives and Measures

Objective	Measure	Type of Measure
To communicate clearly and effectively in forms and styles appropriate for the communications professions, audiences, and purposes they serve.	Entrance test on grammar, punctuation, and spelling for Writing for the Media course	Direct
To communicate clearly and effectively in forms and styles appropriate for the communications professions, audiences, and purposes they serve.	Rating of numerous writing examples during the Writing for the Media course to demonstrate student competency in organizing and presenting information in appropriate, correct news style.	Direct Note: A standard syllabus requiring certain types of writing to be taught and evaluated is used.
To communicate clearly and effectively in forms and styles appropriate for the communications professions, audiences, and purposes they serve.	Using a checkoff sheet, communication skills are assessed by faculty and professionals in capstone courses.	Indirect
To communicate clearly and effectively in forms and styles appropriate for the communications professions, audiences, and purposes they serve.	Evaluation of student performance on professional communication tasks at internship by intern provider using a standard rubric.	Indirect Note: Results are tabulated by the School's internship coordinator.
To understand a core of fundamental concepts, values, and skills that include strategy development, critical thinking, problem solving, and understanding the ethical and legal implications of the media and communication industries.	Rating by faculty and professionals of student's ability to demonstrate successful problem solving, critical thinking, and strategic planning and execution, as well as student ability to use channels of mass communications in a responsible and ethical manner in capstone courses.	Direct Note: Each capstone course has a standard rubric that is used for all sections.

Objective	Assessment Method	Type
To understand a core of fundamental concepts, values, and skills that include strategy development, critical thinking, problem solving, and understanding the ethical and legal implications of the media and communication industries.	Through questions on a final exam in the Mass Media Ethics course, rating student ability to think critically, analyze ethical dilemmas, and solve ethical problems.	Direct Note: Each Mass Media Ethics course includes similar questions for measurement on the final exam.
To understand a core of fundamental concepts, values, and skills that include strategy development, critical thinking, problem solving, and understanding the ethical and legal implications of the media and communication industries.	Through questions on a final exam in the Mass Media Law course, rating student understanding of the role media play in society and the importance of First Amendment rights in a democratic society.	Direct Note: Only one section of Mass Media Law is taught each semester, so there are no issues of standardization of exam questions.
To apply tools and technologies appropriate for the communications profession in which they work.	Through College of Humanities and Sciences SmartForce testing, assessing students' basic computer competency in word processing, file management, and Internet use.	Direct
To apply tools and technologies appropriate for the communications profession in which they work.	Rating of student's basic competency in the technology skills needed in each specialty—advertising, public relations. print journalism, and broadcast journalism—made by faculty using a scoring rubric or checklist.	Direct Note: This technology testing is done in courses in the sophomore, junior, and senior years.

School believes that the measures developed at a programmatic level—by the entire faculty—are valid direct measures of student comprehension and application of material and application of skills. Faculty agree on criteria and standards and so set a level of expected performance by which they will judge actual performance. They directly examine student performances rather than ask about them in some way. As Huba and Freed (2000) suggested, we can perform programmatic assessment by gathering data from faculty assessments embedded in courses. For a discussion of the actions taken as a result of findings for several of the measures, see the Appendix.

HOW WE MEASURED THE MEASURES

It was important for the faculty to create measures, beyond the course grades, with which to assess achievement. Check sheets, using a five-part rubric, were developed by faculty who taught the specific courses. These check sheets provide faculty with an efficient way to measure and report student achievement. The check sheets are then turned into the School's Assistant Director who compiles the information.

After going through 1 academic year cycle, it was apparent that some of the check sheets were not as closely aligned to the measures on *WEAVEonline*™ as they should be. The School's Assessment Committee edited the sheets during the 2003 to 2004 academic year and will do so annually. A sample of the measurement checkoff sheets can be found in Fig. 24.1.

CONCLUSION

The School's assessment process is constantly being revisited, as good assessment programs should. During the 2003 to 2004 academic year, the faculty closely examined both the measures and outcomes to make certain that they accurately reflect the School's new curriculum which went into effect in fall 2003, and as noted earlier, edited the measure checkoff sheets. The faculty is also examining whether the measures are appropriately difficult, because all but one were achieved. As the School prepares for its ACEJMC accreditation self-study in 2004 to 2005 and for its accreditation site visit in 2005 to 2006, it feels confident that going through the assessment process using VCU's WEAVE approach has prepared the unit for the assessment portion of accreditation as well as for ongoing evaluation of its curriculum and instruction.

News-Editorial Capstone Course Assessment

(Used for measure 5.)

	Excellent	Very Good	Adequate	Satisfactory	Not Satisfactory
	Demonstrates superior understanding and application of concepts	Demonstrates strong knowledge but application is not consistently outstanding	Minimal ability to grasp and apply concepts	Minimal ability that includes obvious deficiencies in some areas	Unable or unwilling to perform
Critical thinking, problem solving, strategic planning					
Conceptualizes stories/projects					
Handles obstacles to story/project development					
Prepares a clear and comprehensive budget, listing the proposed elements of the story or project					
Research					
Gathers, analyzes and distills information from a variety of appropriate and authoritative sources					
Obtains background information in paper and digital formats when needed					

FIG. 24.1. *(Continued)*

	Excellent	Very Good	Adequate	Satisfactory	Not Satisfactory
Obtains appropriate government records using Freedom of Information laws if necessary					
Plans and executes interviews with diverse sources; asks questions beyond the obvious; balances stories appropriately					
Writing					
Writes clearly and effectively, in a variety of styles (hard news, features, long form, infographic, etc.)					
Editing					
Has mastered AP style					
Produces copy free of spelling, grammatical and punctuation errors					
Checks facts before publication					
Ethics and law					
Understands and applies legal and ethical guidelines					
Execution					
Meets deadlines					

FIG. 24.1. *(Continued)*

Public Relations Campaigns Capstone Course Assessment

(Used for measure 5.)

	Excellent	Very Good	Adequate	Barely Adequate	Not Adequate
	Demonstrates superior understanding and application of concepts.	Demonstrates strong knowledge but application is not consistently outstanding.	Minimal ability that includes obvious deficiencies in some areas.	Minimal ability that includes obvious deficiencies in some areas.	Unable or unwilling to perform.
Problem Solving					
Generates primary and secondary research for client campaign.					
Works within a group to manage time, deadlines and results.					
Critical Thinking					
Based on research, identifies primary and secondary public relations objectives.					
Derives appropriate solutions to public relations objectives.					
Identifies persuasive arguments in support of conclusions and recommendations.					

FIG. 24.1. *(Continued)*

	Excellent	Very Good	Adequate	Barely Adequate	Not Adequate
Strategic Planning					
Creates public relations campaign using the four-step process.					
Develops a plan, timeline and budget for the campaign.					
Identifies appropriate evaluation tools					
Execution					
Makes a formal presentation of the campaign to a panel of judges.					
Develops a plan, timeline and budget for the campaign.					

FIG. 24.1. *(Continued)*

Advertising Campaigns Capstone Course Assessment

(Used for measure 5.)

	Excellent	Very Good	Adequate	Barely Adequate	Not Adequate
	Demonstrates superior understanding and application of concepts.	Demonstrates strong knowledge but application is not consistently outstanding	Minimal ability to grasp and apply concepts.	Minimal ability that includes obvious deficiencies in some areas.	Unable or unwilling to perform.
Problem Solving					
Generates primary and secondary research for assigned product, category, media and consumer information.					
Works within a group to manage time, deadlines and results.					
Critical Thinking					
Based on research, identifies primary and secondary marketing objectives.					
Derives appropriate solutions to communications objectives.					
Identifies persuasive arguments in support of conclusions.					

FIG. 24.1. *(Continued)*

	Excellent	Very Good	Adequate	Barely Adequate	Not Adequate
Strategic Planning					
Creates integrated communications program to be defended.					
Anticipates sales objections and answers them.					
Execution					
Creates an integrated campaign that includes a market overview, consumer information, strategic analysis, media recommendations and creative executions.					
Creates a "campaign book" that includes all relevant information presented in a finished style.					
Creates advertising and other communication for the campaign.					
Makes a formal presentation of the campaign to a panel of judges.					

FIG. 24.1. *(Continued)*

Broadcast Journalism Capstone Course Assessment

(Used for measure 5.)

	Excellent	Very Good	Adequate	Satisfactory	Not Satisfactory
	Demonstrates superior understanding and application of concepts	Demonstrates strong knowledge but application is not consistently outstanding	Minimal ability to grasp and apply concepts	Minimal ability that includes obvious deficiencies in some areas	Unable or unwilling to perform
Critical thinking, problem solving, strategic planning					
Conceptualizes stories/projects					
Handles obstacles to story/project development					
Prepares a clear and comprehensive outline, listing the proposed elements of the story or project					
Research					
Gathers, analyzes and distills information from a variety of appropriate and authoritative sources					

FIG. 24.1. *(Continued)*

	Excellent	Very Good	Adequate	Satisfactory	Not Satisfactory
Obtains background information in paper and digital formats when needed					
Obtains appropriate government records using Freedom of Information laws if necessary					
Plans and executes interviews with diverse sources; asks questions beyond the obvious; balances stories appropriately					
Writing					
Writes clearly and effectively					
Editing					
Has mastered linear and or non-linear video editing					

FIG. 24.1. *(Continued)*

	Excellent	Very Good	Adequate	Satisfactory	Not Satisfactory
Ethics and law					
Understands and applies legal and ethical guidelines					
Execution					
Meets deadlines					

FIG. 24.1. Examples of check off grids used to assess students in capstone courses.

REFERENCES

Accrediting Council on Education in Journalism and Mass Communications. (2004). *Journalism and Mass Communications Accreditation (2004–2005)*. Lawrence, KS: Author.

Commission on Colleges of the Southern Association of Colleges and Schools. (2004). *Principles of accreditation: Foundations for quality enhancement*. Decatur, GA.

FranklinCovey Co. (2003). Quotation on September Monticello daily planning pages (*"Monthly Focus: Productivity—You reap what you sow. Are your efforts bringing forth the desired results?"*).

The Higher Learning Commission/NCA. (2003). *Assessment of student academic achievement: Assessment culture matrix*. Retrieved March 20, 2005, from http://www.ncahigherlearningcommission.org/resources/assessment/AssessMatrix03.pdf

Huba, M. E., & Freed, J. E. (2000). *Learner-centered assessment on college campuses*. Boston, MA: Allyn & Bacon.

Ketchum Public Relations. (1997) *Views of print and broadcast media executives toward journalism education.*

APPENDIX

Findings and Actions Taken for Several Measures

1. Entrance testing for *Writing for the Media* course (covers grammar, punctuation and spelling proficiency).

Criteria for Success (target levels)

Passing level is 55%. Expect 50% to pass on first try; expect 70% to pass on second try.

Findings in 02–03:

50% of students passed the test on the first try; of those taking the test for a second time, 50% passed. Those not passing on the second try often took more than four times to pass.

Action: As a result of these findings, a study was done to determine if the entrance exam was a good predictor of student success in the *Writing for the Media* course. A comparison of student scores on the entrance exam, student cumulative grade point averages and semester grades for the *Writing for the Media* course revealed that a student's GPA (grade point average) was a better predictor of success in the course. As a result, the faculty decided to no longer administer the entrance exam, using instead a 2.25 GPA requirement and the completion of English 101 and Mass Communications 101 with at least a C as the entrance requirement. This was effective in fall 2003. (Note: the School requires a cumulative GPA of 2.25 for entrance into the major as a sophomore or junior. The *Writing for the Media* course is taken as a pre-major.)

2. Rating of numerous writing examples during the *Writing for the Media* course to demonstrate that students understand how to organize and present information in appropriate, correct news style, and their writing is of substantial quality.

Criteria for Success (target levels)

Expect 10–15% to be excellent; 10–15% very good; 50% adequate; 10% barely adequate; 5–10% not adequate.

Findings in 02–03:

Writing: 13% excellent; 44% very good; 31% adequate; 13% barely adequate.

AP style: 25% excellent; 19% very good; 50% adequate; 6% barely adequate.

Action: None taken since achievement fell within expected levels.

3. Communication skills assessment by faculty and professionals, done in capstone courses.

Criteria for Success (target levels)

Assessment will measure to what degree a student's communication skills are at a level comparable to what would be expected of an entry-level employee in this field. Expect 15–20% to be excellent; 15–20% to be very good; 40–50% to be adequate; 5–15% to be barely adequate or not adequate.

Findings in 02–03:

Excellent 43%; Very Good 50%; Adequate 3%; Barely Adequate 3%.
Action: None taken since achievement exceeded expected levels.

4. Internship evaluation of students on professional communication tasks, done by intern supervisors and faculty.

Criteria for Success (target levels)

Assessment will measure to what degree are the student's communication skills at a level comparable to what would be expected of an entry-level employee in this field.

Expect: 15–20% to be excellent; 15–20% to be very good; 40–50% to be adequate; 5–15% to be barely adequate or not adequate.

Findings in 02–03: (based on a random sampling)

Excellent: 30%; Very good: 40%; Adequate: 20%; Barely or not adequate: 10%

Action: None taken since achievement exceeded expected levels.

5. Rating of student's ability to demonstrate successful problem solving, critical thinking and strategic planning and execution, as well ability to use channels of mass communications in a responsible and ethical manner by faculty and professionals in capstone courses.

Criteria for Success (target levels)

50% of students will be judged as having excellent or very good skills; 40% will be judged as having adequate or barely adequate skills; 10% will have below adequate skills. These skills are measured through various assignments and projects in capstone courses. Faculty then rank student achievement using a check sheet.

Findings in 02–03:

Excellent or Good: 80%

Adequate or Barely Adequate: 20%

Action: None taken since achievement exceeded expected levels.

6. Through questions on a final exam in the Media Ethics course, rating student ability to think critically, analyze ethical dilemmas and solve ethical problems.

Criteria for Success (target levels)

90% of students are expected to pass the comprehensive final exam; 90% of students will pass the course.

Findings in 02–03:

93% of students passed the final exam; 96% passed the course.

Action: None taken since findings exceeded objectives.

7. The Law course specifically measures student understanding of the role media play in society and the importance of First Amendment rights in a democratic society.

Criteria for Success (target levels)

Expect 90% of students to successfully answer 60% of questions designed to measure these concepts.

Findings in 02–03:

90% of the students got at least 65% of the material correct across the two exams.

Action: None taken since findings met objectives.

8. Through College of Humanities and Sciences SmartForce testing, student's basic computer competency in word processing, file management and Internet use are assessed.

Criteria for Success (target levels)

Students will be required to pass the Humanities and Sciences required SmartForce tests (*Mircosoft Office Beginning Word* and *Basic IT Concepts*) before being admitted to the School's Upper Division. Expect 50% of students will pass tests on the first try; 75% on the second try.

Findings in 02–03:

Because the test is administered by another unit, it was difficult to determine the number of times it took for students to successfully pass the tests. However, the School's student services coordinator, who oversees admission into the Newswriting course, diligently enforced the prerequisite requiring students to pass the computer competency test before admission into the course.

9. Rating of student's basic competency in the technology skills needed in each specialty—advertising, public relations, print journalism and broadcast journalism will be made by faculty using a scoring rubric/checklist.

Criteria for Success (target levels)

Expect 30% of students will be rated excellent or very good; 45% will be adequate; 25% will be barely or below adequate.

Finding in 02–03:

40% of students were rated as excellent or very good; 50% adequate; 10% barely or below adequate.

Action: Faculty teaching skills-based courses and those that are technology intensive are working toward more stringent standards and testing to ensure that students have appropriate technological skills.

25

Zayed University

Janet Hill Keefer
School of Journalism and Mass Communication
Drake University

> *We're flying this plane while we're building it.*
> —Dr. B. Dell Felder, Provost, Zayed University (1999–2003)

Dr. Felder's analogy, although terrifying, was apt for this upstart start-up university for Emirati women. Students started coming in 1998 to Zayed University (ZU), before all the faculty had been hired, before curricula were established, and before assumptions could be tested. It was a heady proposition: Educate Arab Muslim women in a university patterned on an American model where English would be the language of instruction. The mission was to create an educated cadre of women to lead this young and oil-rich country through the next phase of its development.

The United Arab Emirates (UAE) is barely 30 years old. It emerged from the former Trucial States that ring the Gulf of Arabia, its development and modernization fueled by the discovery of oil. Seven Emirates, all with considerable autonomy, make up the country. The federal capital is Abu Dhabi, which is also the Emirate with most of the oil. Dubai is the tourism and commercial epicenter. The other five Emirates are less developed than either Dubai or Abu Dhabi. The UAE Ministry of Planning estimates that the country's population at the end of 2003 was 4 million. Dr. Joseph Keefer of ZU's Institute for Socio-Economic Research estimates that the Emirati population at the end of 2003 was 750,000—19% of the total population, meaning that about 81% of the people who live in the UAE are expatriates imported to do almost all of the country's work.

The country is seeking to take more control of its own destiny by edu-cating and developing its own citizens' skills so that they can replace the expatriates in most sectors of the country's economy. To that end, ZU was created as a public university based on a Western—primarily American—model. It was created to serve women. Emirati men are more easily able to go abroad for education, although it is probable that a campus for men will open at ZU within a decade.

WHO, WHAT, WHEN, WHERE, AND HOW

The UAE federal government established the institution by decree in 1998 and named it for the country's founding president, Sheikh Zayed bin Sultan al Nahayan. It has "separate but equal" campuses in Abu Dhabi and Dubai led by a single administration. The University gradu-ated its first class in the spring of 2002. ZU currently enrolls approxi-mately 2,100 National women and is a much smaller university than was envisioned at its founding. With the opening of a new campus in Dubai in 2006, enrollments there are expected to increase to 5,000 students. Plans are in development now for a new campus in Abu Dhabi, which is already operating at capacity.

According to a recent study completed by College of Communication and Media Sciences (CCMS) faculty members Tim Walters, Susan Swan, and Ron Wolfe, about three quarters of the fathers and mothers of CCMS students had completed high school or less. Fewer than one in four of the students came from families in which both parents had a high school education or more. Only 4% came from families in which both parents had college degrees (Walters, Swan, Wolfe, Whiteoak, & Barwind, 2004, p. 4). ZU students are more often than not the first women in their families to go to college.

OUTCOMES AS THE FOUNDATION

From the beginning, ZU decided that its academic program model would be based on learning outcomes. The program would focus on students rather than teachers. It would tie outcomes and technology to-gether. ZU could begin this way. Nothing had to be grafted on to aging rootstock. The driving force behind ZU's outcomes-based academic program model was Provost Dell Felder, who recognized from the be-ginning that ZU's graduates had be able to perform and to think through the challenges that will face the country. They would have to stand up against cultural and family pressures to do so. It made sense, then, to embrace a strategy of education that would focus on doing as well as knowing. As Dr. Felder put it, "Knowledge alone is not enough. You have to apply it in changing circumstances. You have to be able to work in a diverse environment" (Wolfe, 2003, p. 16).

In the spring of 2000, a task force of faculty and staff was established to design an academic program that would produce graduates who could meet the needs of the UAE for leaders; that would integrate liberal and professional studies; that "would encourage pedagogy engaging students in interactive, collaborative and applied learning experiences; and encourage the use of technology to enhance teaching and learning" (Zayed University, 2002, p. 11).

The resulting program focuses on five University learning outcomes (ZULOs) and Major Learning Outcomes (MALOs). The ZULOs are as follows: Information and communication literacy, information technology, critical thinking, leadership and teamwork, and global studies.

The University has developed an elaborate system of introducing and assessing the learning outcomes. Students are required to take three courses in Learning Outcomes Assessment (LOA 101, 201, and 300), worth a total of 4 semester credit hr. In this series of courses, students must create an electronic portfolio of evidence to show their achievement of the learning outcomes. Each student must write and reflect about her own experiences in reaching the appropriate level of accomplishment in each of the outcomes. Faculty from across the University are trained in assessment techniques and are assigned to work with students in developing these portfolios, and still other members of all faculties take turns in evaluating them. The practice is to assign students faculty from their own colleges as instructors in the LOA classes, but the match might not always be possible.

The University has learned that the costs associated with this labor-intensive learning and assessment strategy are quite high, and it is currently seeking ways to maintain the effectiveness of the process while reducing the costs. It is likely that more of the University and Major learning outcomes will become embedded in courses while efforts are made to continue to work with students in the self-reflective process.

ZU revised its general education program in the fall semester of 2003. It has moved away from a typical "menu-driven" program in which students could choose courses from all the colleges that met "domain" requirements—such as arts and humanities, or creative expression—to compile sufficient credits to meet general education requirements. It has moved to a new 65-credit-hr program that is characterized by linked courses in broad, interdisciplinary, subject areas and continues through much of the student's career at ZU. This Colloquy in Integrated Learning is designed in part to increase student focus on the learning outcomes. During their freshman and sophomore years, students enroll in core courses that provide an intellectual experience they share with all ZU students and that will draw attention explicitly to one or more learning outcomes. Through a series of closely related interdisciplinary courses, students will develop their abilities in critical thinking, computer applications, information literacy, English, and Arabic. The new curriculum increases the emphasis on writing and critical thinking.

The University has established four levels of accomplishment for each of the ZULOs by which students are measured: beginning, developing, accomplished, and exemplary.

OUTCOMES AND THE COLLEGE OF COMMUNICATION AND MEDIA SCIENCES

The University's five colleges[1]—Arts and Sciences, Family Sciences, Business Sciences, Education, Information Systems and Communication and Media Sciences—determine their own learning outcomes and decide what levels of achievement students must reach in each one. This chapter focuses on the CCMS approach to assessing learning outcomes.

The CCMS's five learning outcomes (discussed later), labeled as competencies, closely parallel those of the University, as Table 25.1 illustrates.

Communication Competence

This learning outcome states that a CMS graduate will be able to write and speak clearly, effectively, and correctly in Arabic and English, appropriately and skillfully adapting the messages to the needs, knowledge, culture, and expectations of her target audience. This outcome is closely tied to the University's information and communication literacy outcome in that both address gathering and presenting information in Arabic and English. The CCMS, in the business of producing professional communicators, has understandably placed heavy emphasis on these outcomes in its courses. It requires three writing courses of all its majors offered within the CCMS—two in English and one in Arabic. Writing

---

[1]In the spring of 2004, the University underwent a reorganization in which one of its six original colleges, the College of Family Sciences, was disbanded as a separate academic entity and its programs and faculty were distributed between the colleges of Arts and Sciences and Education.

TABLE 25.1
Learning Outcomes

Zayed University Learning Outcomes	College Learning Outcomes
Information and communication literacy	Communication competence
	Information literacy and acquisition
Information technology	Technological competence
Critical thinking and reasoning	Task performance and competence
Global awareness–teamwork and leader-ship	Professionalism

and oral presentations are also carefully evaluated in its internship and capstone courses.

Information Literacy and Acquisition Competence

This learning outcome states that a CMS graduate will be able to identify appropriate information sources, effectively gather data, and apply critical thinking skills to effectively analyze the information obtained. This outcome goes along with Communication Competence because it really is impossible to separate the ability to find and retrieve good information from the ability to convey it effectively in speech and writing. It is formally introduced to students in the CCMS in COM 204, Information Gathering, which addresses basic primary and secondary research methods and tools, including the tools of the reporter: interviewing, observation, and web searching.

Technological Competence

This learning outcome states that a CMS graduate will be able to use a variety of technologies to produce effective communication and media-related products, layouts, and messages. The University's analogous outcome, Information Technology, is leading toward an expectation that all ZU graduates will have the computer skills associated with the International Computer Drivers License, which is highly valued in the UAE. The CCMS's outcome of Technological Competence addresses the more specialized technologies students will need to work in such careers as newspaper or magazine editing and design, video production, TV or radio news or production, or web design. Thus, the CCMS expects students to be competent in using software and hardware appropriate to the professional path they wish to follow. Requirements for all students to complete a course in information design mean that all of them should be able to use desktop publishing software, for example, but only students who have taken video production courses need to be conversant with digital video editing software. Training and measurement of success in these technological competencies are primarily handled in courses in information design, photojournalism, video production, infographics, and so forth. Additional assessment is possible during the capstone experience.

Task Performance Competence

This learning outcome states that a CMS graduate will be able to work both independently and collaboratively to execute responsibilities and tasks associated with her chosen profession competently and effectively. The CCMS views this outcome as being closely related to and dependent on a student's ability to think critically in the context of analyzing situations or problems and coming up with solutions. But it also goes to a much less nebulous notion of trying to determine whether students really can perform the tasks associated with their major. Can she write a competent news story or news release? Can she lay out a brochure? Can she shoot and edit a video project? Can she develop an integrated communication campaign? Her instructors in the courses in which the skills are introduced and taught offer the first line of assessment in this outcome, but the internship preassessment and postassessment process and the grading and evaluation process in the capstone courses also provide an opportunity to further evaluate this outcome.

Professionalism

This learning outcome states that a CMS graduate will exhibit professionalism in her chosen field, as reflected in her work ethic, behavior, and interactions. We've found that assessing this outcome is as difficult for us as it was for the U.S. Supreme Court to identify pornography: it's hard to define, but we know it when we see it. The chart in Appendix A lists some indicators of professionalism.

Some of them, such as punctuality, attendance, and meeting deadlines, are easy enough to measure. The University's stringent attendance policy, whereby students are "carded" on entering and leaving the campus every day, helps the CCMS get the message across that attendance and punctuality are important to academic and professional success. It's easy enough to determine when someone is present, whether she arrived on time, and whether she met her deadline for an assignment. All professors in all courses pay close attention to these things, and intern supervisors in the workplace also keep track of attendance, punctuality, and success in meeting deadlines. But some of the others, such as "positive attitude," tact, and ethical behavior, may not be directly measurable. Nevertheless, the CCMS believes it is important to list and emphasize such qualities to illustrate their importance in developing successful careers. Certainly the complete absence of any or all of these is quite noticeable to even the most casual observer. The CCMS sees its Professionalism outcome as related to the University's Teamwork and Leadership outcome, both of which can be assessed through the student's performance in an internship and in her capstone.

ASSESSING STUDENTS

The CCMS uses several assessment tactics, but it places heaviest reliance on two major assessment "moments." One comes just before the student goes to her internship, which usually corresponds closely to the time when her portfolio is assessed in LOA 300. The second comes with the completion of her capstone experience.

The University requires all students to complete an internship, which may be either 10 weeks of full-time work or 20 weeks of half-time work, for which she receives 6 credits. These internships are structured and monitored more carefully than is typically the case in the United States. The CCMS has a faculty member who is assigned a course equivalent for administering the internship program, which includes the semester-by-semester administration of internship assignments and location and developing new ones. Other members of the CCMS faculty act as supervisors of individual students once they are working at their internship placements. The supervisors visit the internship sites at least three times during the duration of the experience, and they assign students various tasks to complete during the course of the internship, which may include keeping a journal or submitting reports to the faculty supervisor while she is on the job.

The formal pre-internship assessment usually takes place in the semester before the internship semester. It focuses primarily on the communication competence outcome. The incoming "class" of interns is assembled and is tested on public speaking, writing, and reporting in English and Arabic. The speaking test requires a student to give short speeches on an assigned topic in English and in Arabic. Speeches are prepared in a classroom setting in a given amount of time. An "audience" of faculty evaluates each student's performance on a set of predetermined criteria, which may include grammatical correctness, assessment of the audience, eye contact, use of appropriate visual aids, use of appropriate information resources, and attribution. The topics of the speeches vary from semester to semester.

The writing test is handled in a similar way: students assemble in a computer lab or classroom, where they are given a topic to research on the World Wide Web. From their research, they are asked to write either a news story or a news release, depending on the major. The stories must be written in both Arabic and English. The stories are distributed among the appropriate faculty for evaluations. If a student turns in a story that her grader believes is borderline, then the faculty member and the internship coordinator review the work to determine the final evaluation.

The CCMS believes that—of all the outcomes identified—communication competence is the one that each student must master at an accomplished level before the internship placement. Any student who does not pass any part of the writing and speaking tests is given remedial help and retested. Only when she demonstrates that she has overcome her deficiencies can she go out for her internship. Students who are found to be ready for internship work then go through a preinternship week of workshops and seminars.

The seminars provide an opportunity to address some of the simplest and most basic things that will be expected in the workplace, such as telephone manners, etiquette within a chain of command, expectations of confidentiality, punctuality, attendance on the job, and other such mundane but important competencies. These topics were identified through feedback from the first group of internship employers. Seminar topics have included the following:

- Making the most of the internship experience.
- Basic office skills.
- Learning objectives to accomplish while Interning.
- Core competencies to develop or improve on the job.
- Following the student Intern guidelines.
- Personal goals statement.
- Professional goals statement.
- Taking responsibility for your Internship experience.
- Shaping your experience to follow your work plan.
- Development of an internship portfolio.
- Workplace expectations.
- Striving for excellence: showing innovation, motivation, and leadership.
- Developing and demonstrating positive work habits.
- Learning to communicate effectively with your employer to get the most out of your experience.

  • Communicating your professional development plans to your supervisor.

A DIFFERENT STARTING POINT IN THE WORKPLACE

ZU students have not had the summer work experience typical of American students. They may have had lots of babysitting experience with their younger brothers and sisters, the average number of which is about six. But they have not worked outside their homes flipping hamburgers, waiting on tables, or checking out groceries at the local supermarket. Research done by CMS faculty members in 2002 showed that fewer than half of the students (47%) had work experience outside the home, and that figure was about twice what it was before the students had come to ZU and was largely the result of the University's own World or Work (WOW) program, which places students in summer jobs. The number of students who take advantage of the program is small. About two thirds of the CCMS's students escape Dubai and Abu Dhabi and the summer heat by going on long vacations to Europe or the Levant (Walters et al., 2004, p. 5).

It is also unlikely that ZU students had any experience working with high school newspapers or other student media. Such activities, by and large, are unavailable in the UAE's public school system. ZU does not yet have a student newspaper, but there is an online radio station on each campus, and some students work for independent study credit on an alumnae magazine edited and produced in the CCMS. This situation will improve, however, within the next year, as the CCMS develops its Zayed Media Lab, a simulated media conglomerate that will eventually publish a magazine, offer television programming, and will devise and create public relations and advertising campaigns and associated work product for internal and external clients.

Employers are surveyed regularly, and the interns' direct supervisors in the workplace evaluate student performance and also provide valuable feedback on what the CCMS curriculum needs to address to better prepare the students for work. The CCMS initiated the practice of a regular survey of employers, but the University's Career Services office now handles the surveying to ensure that a given employer—who may host students from more than one college—is not inundated with questionnaires. The results of these surveys are shared with all colleges.

During the prep week, each student develops a work plan against which she measures her experience after her internship is over. She outlines a set of specific goals for herself, and she is encouraged to share those goals with her direct supervisor at the job site before she begins her work.

Although it is not a universal requirement, many internship supervisors assign students to keep journals while they are on the job. The journals are often useful when students prepare their reflective week presentations. The self-reflecting week is of major importance to students and faculty. The students often invite their internship employers to their presentations, which are often done in Microsoft PowerPoint® and include "Show and Tell" items that the student worked on during the internship.

It is hard to describe these presentations in a way that can do them justice. The students return from their work experience filled with confidence and with a level of self-awareness and professionalism they never would have imagined 8 weeks before when they were preparing to go out on their internships. The presentations are designed to be consistent in content. Each student is given 15 min to answer the following questions: What did you expect of your internship when you began? Did the experience meet your expectations? What do you think were your greatest strengths on your job? What were your greatest weaknesses? What was your most important or memorable experience on the job? What was your greatest disappointment? What suggestions do you have for improving the internship experience? Should the CCMS continue to send interns to this work site? Why or why not? Were you offered permanent employment at your work site? Would you accept a job there if it were offered? Why or why not? Do you expect to get a job after graduation?

The answers to these questions require the student to consider many aspects of her placement and her interest in finding employment outside the home after she completes her studies. They also help the CCMS determine where gaps exist in the students' pre-internship experience. In fact, feedback from students and from employers caused the CCMS to explore lengthening the internship from 10 weeks of full-time employment to 20 weeks of half-time employment. Almost all of the returning interns have said they didn't think the experience was long enough for them to really contribute or to get a real sense of what it would be like to work for a given company or ministry. At this writing, the CCMS is the only college offering a 20-week internship option.

Employers are asked to evaluate the intern's performance using an evaluation form, which helps the faculty supervisors to evaluate the student's work and assign a grade. Employer evaluations also give the CCMS an instrument by which to get an idea of what needs to be added to the curriculum or to individual courses to counteract a deficit. One finding was in the nature of a "roof leaks can be detected in the rain" discovery: students needed more work in writing in Arabic. We addressed the need by working with the Department of Arabic and Islamic Studies to add a 3-credit course in professional writing in Arabic. We expect the new emphasis on Arabic writing in the Colloquy program to be helpful in improving students' Arabic writing and speaking skills.

College faculty have done extensive research on our students, replicating studies of learning styles and life values done on students in the United States. These studies showed that, although great progress has been made, much remains to be done. The data showed clearly that inexperience with the workplace and workplace environment helped create and magnify difficulties. From merely commuting to work to managing relationships to workplace atmosphere, their students' collective naïveté made successful adaptation to work stressful and difficult. Students, although loath to admit it directly, were uncomfortable with such basics as men in the workplace, the distractions of multiculturalism, and the hurly-burly, high-energy directness of private companies (Walters et al., 2004).

Employers are generally extremely pleased and surprised by ZU students' performance. They tell us that our students are self-starters, that they devise projects to keep themselves busy when the employer may not have much for them to do. (This happens much more frequently in the UAE than in the United States. Employers are less experienced in working with interns than are their American counterparts.) Employers also say they find students' writing, speaking, problem-solving, and software skills more than satisfactory. They frequently comment that ZU students' work ethic is more highly developed than is typical of most entry-level Emirati employees.

The CCMS has found that feedback on individual students is also helpful in spotting strengths and weaknesses of the program. For example, several employers of students in the first and second internship placement periods mentioned—in various ways—that students had no idea how to use the telephone for business purposes. This was surprising, because ZU students often have several mobile telephones and seem to use them with carefree abandon, although the University forbids students to use mobiles on campus. Nevertheless, when we questioned returning interns and current students about how to make business calls, we found that, indeed, they had no idea of how to answer a business telephone. Instead of saying, "Good afternoon, this is the National Bank of Dubai's Public Information Office. My name is Huda. How may I help you?" more often than not, they'd simply say "Hello," if they answered the phone at all. Some said they were "afraid" to answer the telephone, so they simply ignored it at work when it rang. Thus telephone etiquette became an important element in prep week discussions.

Another assessment opportunity associated with the internship experience is the professional portfolio each student must prepare before she visits her potential internship employer for the first time. The task of helping interns create their portfolios has usually fallen to the internship coordinator. However, now that the outcomes assessment process has matured and yielded extensive electronic academic portfolios for each student, that task is likely to shift to a one-credit assessment course that will help the student develop her professional portfolio from her learning outcomes portfolio. This assessment provides an opportunity for the CCMS to see what the student has accomplished in creating her outcomes portfolio and can provide insight into the student's writing and critical thinking skills as well, although enrollment at the University now is small enough to allow faculty to get to know students as individuals very quickly. This assessment course began in the spring semester of 2004. The items the CCMS expects to be included in each student's pre-internship portfolio are listed in Appendix B.

The CCMS moved from pass–fail grading of the internship to the A–F grading scheme. The internship coordinators and faculty supervisors wanted a better way to mark different levels of student performance in internships and were satisfied that they had credible ways of discerning what those differences were, thanks to continuing close contacts between faculty supervisors and workplace supervisors and the interns themselves. An outline of the 2000-point grading scheme is illustrated in Table 25.2.

Capstone: Tying It All Together

Each senior at ZU must complete a capstone experience aimed at topping off and tying together all the threads of her college career—her coursework, her internship experience and her extracurricular activities. Capstones are supervised by faculty, but the students themselves are largely responsible for the design and implementation of their own projects. The project should require that each student address the learning outcomes identified by her college major. These projects are also supposed to call on the student to perform the specific tasks associated with her professional skills set. Capstone Festivals on each of the campuses provide an opportunity for the communities inside and outside the University to see and assess students' work.

The University's president, Sheikh Nahayan Mubarak Al Nahayan, Minister of Higher Education and Scientific Research, sets great store by the capstone concept and experience. He attends the festivals each year, and said at the first one, which was held in June of 2002, "Capstone projects are tangible outcomes of the educational model of Zayed Uni-

TABLE 25.2
Point System

Prep Week	
Attendance: 100 points per day (5 × 100)	500
Employer research	100
Portfolio submitted and approved	200
Internship	
Attendance	200
Midterm evaluation by employer	100
Final evaluation by employer	200
Biweekly reports	400
Reflective week presentation	300
Total Points Possible	
	2000

Letter grades for internships will be based on the points accumulated above:
    1800–2000 = A
    1600–1799 = B
    1400–1599 = C

Students who earn fewer than 1,400 points must repeat the internship. Bonus points may be awarded to students who submit projects or work completed as part of the internship. These points may be awarded at the discretion of the faculty internship supervisor.

versity. They represent a good example where students and faculty are joining together in a very important learning experience" (Capstone Festival Speech, June 9, 2002, Dubai). "Students learn to focus on their academic discipline from a holistic perspective, and they learn to integrate various elements of their academic training," he added, noting that the projects also help students make the transition from college to career.

"I look to the Capstone experience to give each student a sense of accomplishment, a sense that her intellectual life has been enhanced and a sense that the university provides her with the best possible learning environment," he said. Sheikh Nayhan's attendance each year at the Capstone Festival is not merely ceremonial. He views the festival and the capstone projects themselves as a major window through which the community can see and assess ZU. He pays close attention to the students' topics, and he makes sure prominent Nationals and expatriates are invited to attend. The U.S. Ambassador has attended the festival in Abu Dhabi, and the Embassy's public affairs and education officers usually attend every year. The Sheikh also serves as president of the University of the United Arab Emirates and chancellor of the Higher Colleges of Technology. It is clear that he uses the Capstone Festivals to compare ZU's performance—through its students' accomplishments—with the other public institutions of higher learning in the country.

In the CCMS, capstones are generally group projects. Because the Integrated Communication major (public relations and advertising) is much larger than News and New Media, most of the CCMS's capstones have involved projects to develop integrated communication campaigns.

Some of the projects go beyond the mere development of the campaign, however, and often include the implementation of a major event that the students identified as a centerpiece of their campaign plans. Some of the events have been fairly spectacular, including one that focuses on the country's late president, Sheikh Zayed. Students collected a wide range of memorabilia and art associated with Sheikh Zayed, secured prime space in Heritage Village in Dubai (a recreation of an Arab town of the early 20th century), and invited dignitaries, including Sheikh Nahayan and Sheikh Abdullah bin Rashid al Maktoum, the Minister of Information and Culture, who—along with about 1.5 million other people—viewed the resulting exhibit, "Sheikh Zayed: A Modern Legend."

Another capstone, which drew about 600 to the Dubai campus, addressed the topic, "Marriage Without Debt," which is a serious concern for young Emiratis and for the government. A marriage of two Nationals easily can cost upwards of $25,000, and often costs much more than that. Young men are expected to provide a substantial dowry to the bride's family, gifts of money, jewelry, a car, a house (which is often subsidized by the government), parties, a honeymoon, and so forth. The country has a Marriage Fund that provides a subsidy of about $20,000 for the wedding. A National man could marry a foreign woman and avoid much of this expense. If a National woman marries a foreigner, she loses her Emirati citizenship and the considerable benefits that go with it. Consequently, National women saw themselves as getting shut out of the marriage market and facing a life of possible spinsterhood.

ZU students decided to address the issue head-on. They planned and implemented an event that included the director of the Marriage Fund, as well as young men from the Higher College of Technology in Dubai to debate with female students the issue of the high cost of marriage. (Bringing National men onto campus was no small achievement. Permission from the University's Vice President, Dr. Hanif Hassan al Qassimi, was required. Cultural mores and University rules strictly separate Nationals of the opposite sex. Men of other nationalities teach at ZU, always aware of strict rules of behavior of men toward female students.) Although the event perhaps generated more heat than light (we can't be sure because all the debate was in Arabic), it was a landmark moment for ZU and its students because of the elements of controversy surrounding the topic and because of the public and academic interaction between men and women.

The government recently announced that National men could no longer take foreign wives, but it is unlikely that there was a cause and effect relation between the capstone project and the subsequent government action. Nevertheless, the students felt that they had at least been able to express their concerns in a highly visible way. This, in itself, was unusual and gratifying to the University community.

Both of these capstone projects generated news coverage in both the English language media and Arabic media. Others have as well, which is what the students strive for, although many of the individual participants shy away from being photographed or even interviewed about their work. Faculty who oversee the projects are less interested in the public visibility of the students' work than in students' performance leading up to the public event itself. They must push the students to pay attention to the posters, publications, news releases, programs, and other collateral materials associated with each event. These kinds of concrete demonstrations of student skills are more important exhibits in the students' professional portfolio than a news story about the event in which the contributions of the individual student is often lost. It is difficult to get the students to see that when they are caught up in the excitement and intensity of carrying off a major event.

Capstones of this sort offer a chance to help students progress toward fulfilling the University's teamwork and leadership outcome, because in such an undertaking, students may have leadership tasks in some areas and team member tasks in others. Teamwork and leadership also tie in to the CCMS's Professionalism outcome.

It is an ongoing challenge for supervising faculty to find ways to get the students themselves to evaluate and rate the performances of their colleagues and to be realistic about their own performances. This is not unusual, of course. Western students and faculty face many of the same issues, but in a tribal society like the UAE, which is a federation of tribes, the phenomenon called *wahsta* complicates matters. Wahsta is associated with the influence attached to a tribal affiliation. Students with little wahsta tend to defer in all things to students with high wahsta. This means that relative wahsta levels influence leadership patterns as well as candor at peer evaluation time. Nevertheless, students learn quickly that their own grades can rise or fall because of underperformance by other team members. Indeed, some teams have "fired" team members who failed to complete tasks or meet deadlines. But an underperforming high-wahsta student would be more likely to be worked around by other members of the team.

Faculty who supervise the group capstone projects have developed strategies to make sure that students are held accountable for discrete elements of their projects. Students are graded on their separate assignments over the course of the semester. Some professors also give exams that are related to specific aspects of the project, and others introduce formal peer evaluation exercises into the projects. At the end, many of the projects face client evaluations and audience evaluations as well.

LESSONS LEARNED

Surveys of employers, examination of student portfolios, employers' evaluations of interns, faculty research on students' values and learning styles, and feedback from students themselves, have suggested several general and specific adjustments in the CCMS's programs. The addition of a special professional writing course in Arabic was one such change, as was the inclusion in prep week of instruction in basic office and workplace behavior. Taken together, all the feedback has indicated that ZU students need far more experience with working itself. In the Walters et al. (2004) study, "Educating Ms. Fatima" (p. 8), 80% of the students surveyed said that they believed ZU had adequately prepared them for the work they were expected to do during their internships. But an even larger percentage—86%—found work to be vastly different from academic work. Walters's study found that students' expectations of working conditions, salary, and interaction with coworkers, were by and large unrealistic.

To help students become more realistic job-seekers on graduation, the CCMS developed Zayed Media Lab (ZML) in hopes of providing a realistic simulation of the work environment while students are still in school. As mentioned earlier, ZML will function as a global media conglomerate in which students will create media products, as well as function as a corporation itself. In that way, students will be able to get necessary experience working on either a newspaper or magazine, working in radio or television, and handling marketing and promotional activities for the various products and services ZML will provide. It is an ambitious undertaking, but one that can be beneficial to students in the CCMS and to the community as well. The CCMS began experimenting with the ZML concept in the spring of 2004 by joining three basic courses (media writing, information design, and information gathering), which were team-taught by two members of the faculty. The classes met back-to-back twice a week, meaning that the students spent 12 contact hr a week working and thinking media. Indications are that the students benefited from the experience.

In the fall of 2003, the CCMS was invited to nominate students to go to the United States for internships in news media during the spring of 2004. The internships were funded by a U.S. State Department grant secured by

Dr. Leonard Teel of Georgia State University. As part of the process of selecting the interns, the CCMS held a day of competition during which students took a practice version of the Test of English as a Foreign Language (TOEFL), wrote a news story from research done online, wrote stories from fact patterns, and wrote a story from information gained during a mock news conference. The practice TOEFL turned out to be a very revealing test that seemed to predict success on the other measures fairly effectively. Both the CCMS and the University are dedicated to the notion of turning out bilingual graduates, so it seems likely that students will be given the TOEFL at some point during the junior year.[2]

CONCLUSION

One of the goals of the CCMS is to become accredited by the Accrediting Council on Education in Journalism and Mass Communication (ACEJMC). This means that the assessment process will soon have to incorporate or adapt the Council's principles of accreditation, which can be incorporated into the CCMS's current learning outcomes. (See ACEJMC Online Information Center, www.ku.edu/~acejmc/ for a listing of the principles of accreditation, core professional values, and suggestions for direct and indirect assessment of student learning.) The current assessment moments at the time of the internship and capstone project will provide opportunities to assess many of these outcomes directly, as will the ZML participation. Others will be incorporated into the course outcomes, where most are already subsumed in the CCMS's modest list of outcomes.

The processes and procedures already in operation in conjunction with the internships are working well. The capstone experience is salutary in its function of tying the threads of a student's education, but the CCMS will need to adopt ways to more carefully document the capstone effectiveness. Student presentations to clients should become more formalized, and a panel of faculty should join with clients in evaluating the students' presentations using an agreed-on checklist of criteria. The incorporation of a TOEFL during the junior year would yield valuable information in time to allow students to get remedial instruction in English if necessary before graduation. A similar test of their prowess in Arabic would also be an important indicator of competence.

The University itself is analyzing its current assessment procedures as it seeks accreditation from the Middle States Association for Higher Edu-

---

[2]Students must score at least 500 on the Test of English as a Foreign Language before entering the baccalaureate program. It is likely that they will be expected to attain a score of 550 on the second test, midway through the baccalaureate degree.

cation. Early discussions suggest that some of the highly individualized assessment that is done now through the LOA courses will shift to the colleges. In the meantime, the CCMS will continue to refine and document its own assessments of student and curricular success. The University and the CCMS are young and well-positioned to adopt the strategies and tactics suggested by ACEJMC as part of a set of routine measurements that are underway now and that will become more elaborate and formal over time.

REFERENCES

ACEJMC Online Information Center. www.ku.edu/~acejmc/

Walters, T., Swan, S., Wolfe, R., Whiteoak, J., & Barwind, J. (2005). *Educating Ms. Fatima*. Al-Raida, in press.

Wolfe, R. (2003, Spring). Farewell Dr. Dell. *Achievers, 1*(2), 14–17.

Zayed University. (2002). *Academic program model, academic year 2002–2003*. Dubai, UAE: Zayed University.

APPENDIX A

Learning Outcomes Descriptions

Communication Competence

On completion of this program, students in the College of Communication and Media Sciences will be able to write and speak clearly and effectively in both English and Arabic, appropriately and skillfully adapting their messages to the needs, knowledge, culture, and expectations of their target audiences.

Indicators	Assessment Criteria	Assessment Venues
Ability to present information clearly, accurately, and effectively through oral, written, and visual communication media	• Clarity • Accuracy • Organization • Proficiency in English and Arabic, written and spoken • Effective use of visual aids • Appropriate form and style • Delivery proficiency	Courses: Media Writing I & II, Writing for Integrated Communication, Print Media Editing, Professional Writing in Arabic, Public Speaking and Professional Presentation, Information Design, Video Production I & II, Capstone Internship Portfolio

(Continued)

Indicators	Assessment Criteria	Assessment Venues
Ability to adapt and tailor information to fit the needs, knowledge, expectations, and culture-related traits of target audiences	• Proficient audience analysis and massage adaptation	Courses: Media Writing I & II, Writing for Integrated Communication, Print Media Editing, Professional Writing in Arabic, Public Speaking and Professional Presentation, Information Design, Video Production I & II, Capstone Internship Portfolio
	• Accurate understanding of relevant cultures and skillful application of intercultural communication principles, thus reflecting an understanding of the diversity of groups in a global society	Courses: Intercultural Communication, Public Speaking and Professional Presentation, Information, Media Law and Ethics, Comparative International News, Capstone

Technological Competence

On completion of this program, graduates of the College of Communication and Media Sciences will be able to skillfully use a variety of technologies, both individually and in convergence with each other, to produce effective communication and media-centered products, layouts, and messages.

Indicators	Assessment Criteria	Assessment Venues
Ability to use a variety of technologies to convey effective visual information and achieve persuasive objectives	• Proficiency in using web, video, audio, and print hardware and software appropriate to the communication professions associated with students' majors, i.e., proficiency in using the following: MS Word MS PowerPoint® Adobe Photoshop® QuarkXpress® Adobe Illustrator® Final Cut Express or Pro Adobe GoLive® Digital still and video cameras • Proficiency in converging two or more of the above software applications or technologies.	Courses: Information Design, Print Media Editing, Video Production I and II, Infographics, Photojournalism, Public Speaking and Professional Presentation, Web Design, Internship Portfolio Capstone

Information Literacy and Acquisition Competence

On completion of this program, graduates of the College of Communication and Media Sciences will be able to identify appropriate information sources, effectively gather data, and apply critical thinking skills to analyze the information obtained.

Indicators	Assessment Criteria	Assessment Venues

Ability to identify appropriate information sources
Ability to conduct research and evaluate information by methods appropriate to the communication professions in which graduates intend to work
Ability to evaluate and edit own work and work of others
	• Use of resources and sources appropriate to given assignments
	• Proficiency in gathering information from the Internet, library, and human sources demonstrating skills in
	  ○ Library research
	  ○ Interviewing
	  ○ Survey development and administration
	  ○ Observation
	    Internet and IT research
	• Proficiency in applying basic numeric and statistical concepts
	• Critical thinking
		Courses: Information Design, Media Writing I and II, Writing for Integrated Communication, Professional Writing in Arabic, Integrated Campaign Planning, Print Media Editing I & II, Portfolio Internship

Task Performance Competence

On completion of this program, graduates of the College of Communication and Media Sciences will be able to work both independently and collaboratively to execute responsibilities and tasks associated with their chosen professions competently and effectively.

Indicators	Assessment Criteria	Assessment Venues

Ability to work independently to successfully accomplish objectives, projects, and tasks	• Demonstrated understanding and application of
	  ○ problem-solving
	  ○ decision-making
	  ○ task-planning
	  ○ task-implementation
	  ○ time-management
	  ○ self-reflection
		Courses throughout the majors will address task performance competence, but evaluation of the internship portfolio and the capstone project will be the places where this outcome will be emphasized most.

(Continued)

Indicators	Assessment Criteria	Assessment Venues
Ability to work collaboratively to successfully accomplish objectives, projects, and tasks	• Demonstrated understanding and application of ○ consensus building ○ appropriate task division ○ positive communication climate skills ○ conflict management ○ effective group problem-solving and decision-making processes	The pre-internship assessment, performed by the internship coordinator, each student's faculty internship supervisor, her workplace supervisor, and other faculty as required for test administration and evaluation, will assess and evaluate. The instructors of record for the capstone courses will take the primary role in assessing and evaluating student performance and assigning grades. Clients will also have a role in assessing capstones, as will the larger audience of the University community, parents, and potential employers.

APPENDIX B

Internship Portfolio Guidelines

Checklist Items

- A resume (a personal photograph is optional).
- An official copy of the student's University transcript.
- A personal statement of goals, plus as many as appropriate of the other items listed later.

College of Communication and Media Sciences Major Learning Outcomes

1. Communication Competence
2. Technological Competence
3. Information Literacy and Acquisition Competence
4. Task Performance Competence
5. Professionalism

The College internship coordinator and internship faculty supervisors evaluate portfolios before students show them to potential internship employers. An approved portfolio is worth 200 points of the internship grade. Students are advised that their portfolios should reflect their very best work and should be completely free of errors.

Item to Be Included	Outcomes Items Should Illustrate	Quality Standards
Personal statement of career goals	1,5	• No mistakes in spelling, grammar, syntax • Clear understanding of positions and their function in the industry for which the portfolio is aimed
Writing samples, such as newspaper clips, press releases, personal profiles, features, broadcast scripts, etc. Include items that have been published or created for real clients, if possible. (Limit number of examples to a maximum of two each)	1,3,4,5	• No mistakes in spelling, grammar, syntax • Appropriate use of sources • Adequate attribution of quotations • Style appropriate to medium, audience, and purpose • Observation appropriate professional and ethical conventions

Samples of photos or illustrations, such as logos, advertisements, posters, or other collateral materials produced for class assignments, clients, clubs, or other extracurricular activities. (Limit number of examples to a maximum of two each)	1,2,3,4,5	• No mistakes in spelling, grammar, syntax
		  • Appropriate use of sources
		  • Examples should meet professional standards of composition, focus, typography, etc.

Samples of any pages designed using computer software produced for class assignments, clients, clubs, or other extracurricular activities. Pages designed for hard copy publications and web pages should be included, but no more than two examples of each. A photo essay of more than one page counts as one example	1,2,3,4,5	• No mistakes in spelling, grammar, syntax • Appropriate use of sources • Examples should meet professional standards of composition, focus, typography, etc.

(Continued)

Item to Be Included	Outcomes Items Should Illustrate	Quality Standards
A program from an event the student planned or in which she participated as part of a class project or campus organization	4,5	Standards of good writing and design should apply if the student had anything to do with the creation or publication of the program itself. Otherwise, the program serves to verify her participation and role in the event and the intended audience of the event
Samples of academic papers, such as research papers, course projects, reviews, bibliographies, essays, analyses, etc. Include no more than two examples	1,3,4	• No mistakes in spelling, grammar, syntax • Appropriate use of sources • Adequate attribution of quotations • Style appropriate to medium, audience, and purpose

- Certificates of awards, scholarships, and honors
- Certificates for special training
- Letters of commendation or thanks from previous employers, organizations, advisers, leaders of projects on which you worked, or faculty advisers.
- Summary reports of evaluations from the World of Work (WOW) or similar activities that indicate on-the-job experience

Assessment of Portfolios

Not all students will include each of the items listed. In addition to the quality standards associated with the portfolio items indicated, the portfolios themselves are assessed using the following criteria:

Overall professional appearance and consistency of look

Presence of appropriate items of acceptable quality

Organization. Examples of work should be captioned and include the circumstances under which each was created. A table of contents is essential.

Variety

Error-free throughout